What peopl

Being Mentally Healthy

in spite of a mental illness

"Elizabeth provides a personal, courageous and talented voice to the subject of mental illness. Her own expertise – living with and in recovery from a mental illness – is much needed to help reduce the stigma experienced by so many individuals in our society. Her husband's first-person perspective is also very insightful. I thoroughly enjoyed reading Elizabeth's story, and applaud her determination in making this book a reality."

– Romie Christie, Manager, *Opening Minds,* the anti-stigma initiative of the Mental Health Commission of Canada

"Though this book is about one woman's battle with schizophrenia, this is a story about mental resilience, not mental illness. It should be required reading for anyone entering a helping profession."

– **Dr. Heather Stuart,** Professor and Bell Canada Mental Health and Anti-Stigma Research Chair, Queen's University, Kingston, Ontario, Canada

"Not just people with mental illnesses and their families, but everyone should learn more about promoting an inclusive society. Elizabeth Anderson's *Being Mentally Healthy in spite of a mental illness* is more than one person's account, but recognition of the fundamental commitment to each other necessary to everyone's health and wellbeing."

- **Sonya Jakubec**, **RN, BHScN, MN, PhD(c)** Associate Professor, Mount Royal University, Calgary

"*Being Mentally Healthy* provides beautifully written and compelling insight into the journey of a courageous woman. Elizabeth shares her journey from illness to wellness allowing the reader a view into her reality – one of truth, hope and inspiration."

– Patricia Winter, PhD

"Elizabeth shares her often agonizing story with honesty and a grace that is very moving. Her deep love for the people in her life, and for life itself, is inspirational to all who have fought the insistent darkness of mental illness."

– Fiona Haynes, Provincial Partnership Education Program Director & Calgary Branch Manager Schizophrenia Society of Alberta, Calgary Chapter

"Elizabeth's book stays with you! Her authentic, hopeful voice echoing back the reality of mental illness offers a workable theory for being healthy and includes her husband's story of love."

– E. Anne Hughson, PhD, Associate Professor Director, Community Rehabilitation and Disability Studies, Faculty of Medicine, University of Calgary

"*Being Mentally Healthy in spite of a mental illness* is a refreshing story that captures the essence of what it means to be mentally ill and how to regain one's mental health. Elizabeth's recipe for success includes a holistic approach to wellness. Being Mentally Healthy is an important book!"

– Laurie Beverley, RN, BN, MN, Executive Director of Primary and Community Care, Addiction and Mental Health, Alberta Health Services

"Elizabeth has learned to catch the wave of mental illness and ride it with joy and skill. Her book will inform and inspire. It is a must read for those who struggle and those who love those who struggle."

– Rev. Scott R. Weatherford, **BA, MRE,** Lead Pastor, First Alliance Church

"Highly recommended reading for anyone even remotely interested in the mental health field. Anderson owns her story with unblemished honesty and courage. A skillful mentor for those suffering from or who know someone with schizophrenia or mental health issues, her fresh, new, insightful voice should be put in the hands of all health care professionals. Well done!"

– Susan Waldie, Community Facilitator Progressive Alternative Society of Calgary

"I have watched Elizabeth make her own journey over the past 18 months and am amazed at her ability to overcome. She is a model of excellence with much to share."

— Perry Rose, **M. NLP,** Author

Being
Mentally
Healthy

in spite of a mental illness

ELIZABETH ANDERSON

Frances Dunbar's graduation photo used with permission of Hilda W. Reiner of Hilda Onions Photography Ltd. / Elizabeth Anderson's graduation photo: Artona permission granted by TJ Rak / Wedding photo used with permission of Sid Helischauer of Dynamic Images www.dynamicimages.ca

Cover design & layout by Julie McPhail.

Cover photograph:
John White / Flikr / Getty Images.

Chapter ending graphic:
1197149679995890649johnny_automatic_crashing_wave.svg.hi
OCAL / clker.com / royalty free public domain clip art

ISBN 978-0-9881071-0-6

Library and Archives Canada Cataloguing in Publication

Anderson, Elizabeth, 1964-
        Being mentally healthy : (in spite of a mental illness) / Elizabeth Anderson.

Includes bibliographical references.
ISBN 978-0-9881071-0-6

        1. Anderson, Elizabeth, 1964- --Mental health. 2. Schizophrenics--Canada--Biography. I. Title.

RC514.A54 2012   616.89'80092   C2012-905481-X

This book is dedicated to my mom,

with the hope that she would be

proud of me.

Contents

Acknowledgements

I would like to thank God for all He has done for me – I say this knowing He will bring you your heart's desires too. In addition, I would like to thank all the people who have had a hand in my success. My heartfelt thanks to:

Lori Eberhardt, Pat Winter and Carla Hamarsnes for their encouragement and for helping me be the best me possible.

Doug, Dave, and Iain and their families for being supportive.

Fay Herrick for being my friend, mentor, confidant and a speaker of truth in my life.

Fiona Haynes for being a strong voice of reason – one who knows when to kick me in the butt and say get going and when to tell me to take it easy and rest.

Deanna Fraudette for being a true friend through thick and thin.

Sonya Jakubec who was an early encourager and the reason I took this project seriously.

Dr. Margo for believing in me.

Perry Rose for being there every step of the way on this journey of becoming an author.

Kathleen Ryan, who was a key person in my regaining my footing after the diagnosis and who continues to be supportive.

Janet Loewen and Wendy Hourd for encouraging me.

Heather Wile for believing I could make a contribution and helping me find the gift of writing.

Scott and Tara Weatherford for believing in me and this project.

Susan Waldie for telling me to quit my job and write.

Marsha for being the kind of person people want to be around even if they are not feeling well.

Andrea for her laugh and for helping me take the next step.

Barb Vogan for her patience and for never giving up on trying to teach me the art of simplicity.

Arlo for his wisdom and tenacious belief that I could do it.

Louise for helping me take the early baby steps in my faith.

Nicole Milton for her kindness and for being the best advocate for my mental health.

Dave and Elsie for their compassion for my plight and for being the nicest people you would ever want to meet.

Stuart and Laura and their family for being understanding and spurring me on.

Miles and Tracey for being so supportive of Wade and me over the years.

Dr. Heather Stuart and Dr. Julio Arboleda-Florez for starting me on the journey of anti-stigma work and for devoting their lives to this cause.

Trish Romanchuk of Blitzprint for walking me through the process.

Cheryl Siebring for help with the final edit.

Julie McPhail for the brilliant graphic design.

Christine Sopczak, a gifted editor, who is absolutely fantastic to work with, and who is a newfound friend.

And especially Wade because he is an extraordinary person.

No one gets to where they are going alone. I have done this with a great group of people surrounding me – you know who you are. You are the best and I am truly blessed.

Foreword

Elizabeth Anderson's book, Being Mentally Healthy in spite of a mental illness, is about her life-changing experiences with a serious chronic mental illness, how these experiences have impacted her life, and how she has managed to effectively maintain good mental health with a positive outlook on life.

In life, human relationships can be and often are difficult; this is true for everyone. The common misconception with regard to people who have mental illness is that their life experiences with relationships are somehow more difficult and more harmful than relationships among the 'mentally healthy' segment of society. Emotional stress caused by human relationships is a common occurrence in life. Elizabeth uses her personal relationships to show that while they may have been difficult they are experiences common to everyone. While mental illness might complicate relationships; it does not need to define them.

The power schizophrenia has to disrupt, disorganize and destroy a person' ability to function in daily life is discussed in Elizabeth's book. Her goal is to present a very clear sense that although the seriousness of mental illnesses cannot be overstated, mental health can be achieved by those who experience serious disorder of the brain.

Elizabeth offers a depth of understanding of schizophrenia and the people who experience it not readily available to the general population. Through the pages of her book, Elizabeth provides a guide to achieving and maintaining good mental health in spite of experiencing a mental illness.

Fay Herrick, friend
Mother of a person who has schizophrenia
Retired Director of Programs and Services
Schizophrenia Society of Alberta

Introduction

At first, the wave that knocked me off my feet seemed innocuous. Its power to overtake me was not readily apparent. Like the wave on the cover, the wave that came my way did not look like a storm wave but it was overpowering. The wave sent my heels skyward and getting back on my feet has taken almost all of my time, energy and will since then. I am back on my feet now and the illness is easier to manage. The crashing waves of symptoms do not knock me down as often or for as long and there are calm periods between the waves.

I know what it is like to be in the midst of a terrible storm and what life is like when the winds die down. Experiencing both extremes has given me a need to tell my story to encourage others. It was a long road back to the functioning I lost and while making sense of what I had been through, I came up with my recipe for success.

I wrote my book to give hope and to give voice to a real experience of getting well.

People with mental illness are not typically given a voice to tell of their experiences and have to deal with the stigma surrounding the diagnosis.

To deal with a mental illness and reduce stigma, people need knowledge.

If you know of someone with a mental illness, my hope is that by reading this book you will better understand them. People who experience schizophrenia need to have the support of many people if they are to overcome the debilitating nature of the illness and manage symptoms successfully.

If you have a mental illness, my hope is that my story will be a beacon of light to help you navigate the storms of mental illness.

For questions to consider when reading the book, refer to the Springboard for Understanding in the Additional Perspectives section. In addition, use the wide margins to write notes as you read.

Chapter 1

The Storm
Before the Storm

I know my mother, who everyone else knew as Frances, was coping the best she could. She was very intelligent, and education was everything to her. She applied for university in Calgary the first year the university opened in 1960. She earned her degree while working full-time as a teacher by taking courses at night and during the summer. Her mom, Elizabeth, whom I was named after, died in 1974 and my mother had just finished grieving when she decided to pursue a Master's degree in education.

Mom had been working with teenagers with developmental disabilities. She helped her students learn to read, which a novel concept and great achievement back in the 70s. She believed she had something important to add to the conversation and was looking forward to another foray into the world of academia.

So, she decided that she, no, *we* needed an adventure. She had a plan. She applied to graduate schools in the Boston area and she and I went down to check them out. I was 12 going on 13 at the end of summer and I was looking forward to becoming a teenager.

If she was accepted, we would live with my aunt. My mom would go to school and in doing so would instil in me a love for education and we would bond. Her reasoning was that if we had a close bond, the coming teenage angst would pass us over. Bonding was an insurance policy against the teenage tiffs. We would be close and it would last the rest of our lives.

I remember packing for the trip to Boston. Aunt Mildred lived right outside Boston – Foxboro, to be exact. Perfect. Everything was perfect. We were excited because not only were we going on a trip, we were going on a real adventure.

The summer plan was that Mom would pick her university and register and then when summer was nearly over, we would go back to Calgary to gather everything we would need to live in Foxboro, Mass, U S of A for a whole year.

My summer in Foxboro was the best of my life. Aunt Mildred happened to have a next door neighour who just happened to have a daughter exactly my age. We were fast friends. It was like we had known each other forever. Her name was Debra* and her best friend, Roberta*, and I were giggly girls trying to face our emerging womanhood with the utmost of grace. My new friends told me I had an accent and I insisted they had the afflicted speech. We got along famously. We swam at the beach and went out for lunch with my mother and Aunt Mildred. I remember my mother asking for clam chowder. Manhattan red was her favourite. I can still smell the aroma of the soup and see Mom enjoying every succulent mouthful.

Some afternoons Roberta, Debra and I would stay in the house and have the best fun. We would play dress up with my aunt's old hats and clothes. We would pretend we were models who were in a New York fashion show and one of us would always announce we had to quit because we were marrying a handsome man who was whisking us away to live in Hawaii.

After a wonderful summer Mom and I returned home to the cool evenings of Calgary. We thought the dream would continue on forever ... but it ended abruptly. My mom got "the news."

It changed her. It changed her life. It changed everything.

Before we left Mom had applied for scholarship money, and when we returned, she inquired about how the money would be dispersed. It was then that she received the news. Good news and bad news. The good news was my mom had better marks which, in her mind, was the only criteria for receiving a scholarship. The bad news

– they picked the other teacher because she was younger. The dream was over. The summer which had held such promise ended with a whimper. My dad was well meaning but managed to say the wrong thing: "That's okay. No big deal, Frances. You can still teach."

To say she was devastated was an understatement. She was only 53 but that day she deemed herself old. She gave up. She did what was essential, like go to work, but after work one glass of wine turned into two. My dad suspected my brother was sneaking a glass of wine but I thought it was all her. The bottle of wine became empty way too early in the week, so Dad stopped buying wine thinking that would solve the problem. But instead it morphed into Mom being swallowed up in a sewage pit of self-pity. She withdrew to her bedroom and from us. I remember when I asked "What happened to Boston?" She replied in a hollow voice, "We are not going back," as she kissed the top of my head wistfully. End of story. Beginning of nightmare.

I felt like I was falling down into a pit with her. I caught her drinking secretly – the bottle was in her bedroom closet. I called a family meeting and told them what I saw. "How could you say that about your mother?" the rest of the family exclaimed disgustedly, as they each stood up, looked at me coldly and left the room. I felt a confusing mixture of bewilderment and loneliness with a hint of anger. I began to question my perception of everything. The anger grew and turned inward and was like a snake that swallowed me whole. I began to feel like it did not matter – and worse – that *I* did not matter. A slow, steady, descent began and I became suicidal. I began to slash my wrists with my dad's razor blades. I was in trouble and everyone was too busy to notice.

The guidance counsellor at school realized I was having problems and informed my parents. As the counsellor suggested, they took me to the hospital where the doctors decided I needed psychiatric help. I spent over a month there trying to figure out how this happened to me. I was in the hospital with kids who came from broken homes or who had been in trouble with the authorities, and kids like me who just had lost the will to live. I was trying to make sense of how I felt or rather why I didn't feel anything except pervasive numbness.

My family had fallen apart and I felt like it was my fault. Somehow, it was *all my fault*. Shame overtook me. It was buried so deep I was unaware of its presence. I thought, "This is all your fault, so no one likes you." I felt deep disgrace that I was not like everybody else. My friend Shelley's* mom told me I just needed a spanking. I was trying to make sense of all of this and when the hospital staff asked me over and over what was wrong I finally yelled back, "I don't know!"

Journal entry - I don't feel good when I am with you and you wonder why I want to be away. I am just the canary who was the first to sense something was wrong.

During that time, two of my brothers were getting divorces and my third brother had dropped out of university. It was major upheaval on top of enveloping sorrow. My mother was emotionally unavailable and it affected all of us. All I could think of at the time was that I must be the flawed one since I was the one spending time in the psych ward. I came out of this experience thinking "I am not fixed."

I was released from hospital, and I knew the shame and sorrow I felt were still with me. Nothing had really changed inside of me. The anxiety I felt in my stomach helped me discover the will I needed. I needed to change something. I adopted a guiding truth – if I am going to be well it is up to me. I often thought this as I tried to navigate through the ensuing storm that was to be my life.

Chapter 2

Brewing Winds

In 1977, in grade seven, I had enrolled in drama. By the time I was depressed in grade nine, it was my only comfort. I loved it. I'd pretend I had no problems and the world was as it should be, and it was, at least while I was in drama class. I went to Provincial Drama School the summer of grade nine and found others with a passion for dramatic art. In grade ten, I was the only junior in the school play cast as an actor. The character I played was drunk at a party and was comedic relief. In grade eleven, I was cast as the female lead in the annual school play. I received an almost perfect grade in Drama 20. The comment that went with the mark was that I should be professional. I wanted to be a drama teacher from that moment on.

A teachers' strike extended the summer of my grade 11 year by two months and I auditioned and was cast in a community theatre project. We work-shopped and adapted a play from the book, <u>10 Lost Years,</u> by Barry Broadfoot.[1] Everyone else in the play worked during the day but because I was the youngest in the play and not in school, I could rehearse with them until 9 pm and did not have to get up in the morning. I met a great group of collaborative artists that summer. We even revived the play for a second run the next September. It was my first time in a community play and it was a very profound experience. Our play was named the best community play for 1980 by the city paper's entertainment columnist. It galvanized my desire to pursue drama as my career. Drama was going well, school not so much.

Everyone I was in high school with knew I had been in the hospital for psychiatric problems in grade nine. The stigma surrounding me because of my mental illness was pretty strong. I had very few friends even though I'd had success in drama. I changed schools in the middle of grade 11, in part to please my mother and in an effort to be happier. I thought if people didn't know I had a mental illness, I would have a better chance at making friends. It did not change the fact that my mom and I were going through teenage wars, and one night, when my dad was out of town, my mom and I had a huge fight. She had been drinking and I had enough, so I moved out. I moved in with a friend of a friend who said it was okay to stay there while I finished high school. I finished high school on time but did not gain the necessary skills to master the next steps I needed to take. My maturity development stopped, which showed up in strange ways.

I had an insidious fear of success that started to creep in. As Mathematics was not my strong suit, I went to summer school after graduating to improve my mark so I could attend university. My mark was 65% and I didn't feel that was good enough, so I did not write the final exam. I took Math

30 a couple more times before I realized I would never be a master mathematician. I did pass Math 30 and was sure I would get into university. In the meantime, I had this crazy idea that I would grow up and be an accountant and become organized. All the people who I thought were "together" were business people and I wanted to grow up and become one of them. I thought if I was good at math, I would be an adult. I didn't realize my gift of creativity was valid. During this time, I did not feel very good about myself and it resulted in me trying to take my own life.

Journal entry - I just saw one of those "feel good because everything is tied up with a nice neat beautiful bow after a convenient two hours" movies. Everyone else's life is like that. My life is not like that. My life will never be like that. I am giving myself no more chances – this is the end of the road.

I was staying at my parents' house and I took every pill in the house which is quite startling since my parents had multiple health issues. I slept that night and awoke in the morning very groggy. My mom phoned an ambulance. I tried to throw up but I couldn't. By the time I reached the hospital, the doctors could do nothing. All the pills had entered my blood stream during the night; there was no point in pumping my stomach. They considered a blood transfusion but were afraid of shock, so my parents had to wait to see if I would live. My mom gave me sponge baths to reduce my fever. In my unconscious state, I was aware I was dying. I bargained with God to let me live. I told Him, "I will serve You if You will grant me this one thing." He sent me back from my travels through a white tunnel. Somehow, my human Godfather was there (even though he was still alive) and made me turn back. He told me, "It is not your time yet." I woke up in the hospital very disappointed. I had given up hope. I had almost made it to heaven and was not happy when I woke up from this suicide attempt. I immediately forgot the promise that I had made to God and the fact I wanted to live, but I did realize on some level that God was in control of things. God is patient. I still felt like a child, in spite of the fact I was 19.

University 1.0

After the suicide attempt and a period of recovery, while waiting to become an adult, I decided I would take drama and become a drama teacher which was, secretly, all I really wanted to do anyway. I applied for university and was accepted.

I arrived on campus in the fall of 1985, excited and nervous and I imagined creative people were interested in collaborating and learning the craft of acting and wanted to play with me. I soon realized this was not the case. I was extremely disappointed. What I found were people with huge egos who wanted to be stars and the atmosphere was not very welcoming. I struggled to go to class and perform. I withdrew from most of my classes halfway through because I couldn't stand the pressure. I stayed in acting but only received a C.

I didn't make friends and I was embarrassed I didn't know more. I didn't realize that is why people go to school; every class teaches people something they don't know. I just know I felt shame: shame about not having friends; shame about not knowing more; shame about not having the skills to navigate university. It was a shock because I hadn't considered the possibility of me not being able to handle post-secondary education. I took other classes but did not find anything else I wanted to do. I was lost. I did not have a plan B.

Journal entry - There is no sense in crying

Overwhelmed unprepared criticized too much new

There is something wrong with me and I can't do it

I can't be a failure

I am smart

I know I am

Consequently, I took a Dean's vacation. The Dean asked me to leave the university after too many F's (Failures) and W's (Withdrawals). However, during my time away from the problems of university, other problems cropped up.

Trouble came in the form of my dad leaving me in 1987. Dad died and it was a shock. My mom had been in the hospital for pancreatitis for almost two months. She was home for a week and we all breathed a sigh of relief. Then, Dad went in to hospital and was scheduled for surgery for an aneurism and died while he waited for the operation. He died in June, just around Father's day.

Journal entry - Grief is an oddity of love. I miss my dad a lot. He said he was proud of me. Why didn't I say something intelligent back? Why did that have to be the last moment?

The advertisements on the radio reminded me I was fatherless. I was only 22. I was not ready. I felt too young, too unprepared.

However, it did make me grow up a bit. I tried to take responsibility for my life. I saw an ad in the paper for free post-secondary education, so I investigated.

On my birthday, the last day of August in 1987, I went to a meeting to see if I would qualify for a new government sponsored pilot project to teach people how to assist with research. The coordinator asked me why I wanted to attend and learn about research. I said I wanted to know about inductive and deductive reasoning. The interview went well and I applied for the program to teach me how to be a research assistant. I was paid to go. Tuition and books were also paid for. I was a professional student.

It was a great experience until Christmas. The denial that my dad had died receded and I was paralyzed. My friends noticed I hadn't returned to school after the Christmas break, so they came to my house. I was about to have a bath when I heard a knock at the door. Bea* and Brenda* stood on my doorstep. Bea insisted, "Get in the car. We will drive you to school." On the way to school, Bea told me, "I will buy you a coffee every morning but you better be here to drink it or I will make you drink it the next day." It was the motivation I needed. I rarely missed a day. When I did miss one day, I was afraid I would have to drink cold coffee the next day but Bea had been away that day too! The course was a full year from September to September including two practicums and I made it through. I had a feeling of long-awaited accomplishment. Things were starting to improve.

I was even getting along with my mother a bit better. I did not realize my mom was sorry I had left home. She had given me a collector's plate for my fifteenth birthday and continued to buy me plates to keep connected to me. We could not be in the same room without a lot of tension but she would phone me and say, "I bought you a plate. Why don't you drop by and get it?" I would go visit her and she would present me with the plate. We tried not to talk about everything that had gone wrong and tried to have a normal mother daughter relationship.

Sometimes she would invite me to go shopping and would buy me clothes. I always felt good at those times. I felt loved for a brief moment in time. We were repairing some of the past damage, so I invited her to my graduation from research school. She offered to pay for university if I wanted to continue.

I thought I was ready to tackle university one more time. I had been successful at the pilot project. I had grieved my dad's death and had carried on in spite of my angst. I had made friends. I was ready. I was sure I could navigate school this time.

Chapter 3

The Makings of a
Perfect Storm

University 2.0

In fall 1989, I arrived on campus and bought
my books. The sheer volume of the reading totally overwhelmed me. I did not go to
class which is the surest way not to succeed.
I was sabotaging myself. It may have been
untreated depression; it may have been fear
of success; it may have been both. I just
could not be on campus. I felt I did not be-
long – my will was not strong enough to
overcome my fears, so I did not get any-
where. I just sat in my apartment knowing
the semester was ticking by. I was not sure
what to do next.

Journal entry - I am mortified about school - what should I do?????? I got a small inheritance from Aunt Mildred. I can use that money to do something about this. Wilderness course or a course where I can fix any problem I have. Which do I choose? I think I should choose the one where I can fix anything, since I don't know what the problem is.

Because of my paralysis and inability to succeed at school, I enrolled in a course advertised on a university bulletin board because it promised to fix everything. I was the least educated, youngest, participant at 24 years old. The course did not deliver the proposed outcomes. The course turned out to be brainwashing. My friend, Lorita*, realized something was desperately wrong when I came home and ripped through my things trying to find my check book to give them more money to reserve my place for the next course before I finished the first one. I was acting out of character. She suggested I not finish the course. "My group bet fifty bucks that I would return the next day," I insisted. "They will lose their money," she stated matter of factly. She was stronger than me mentally and kept me distracted, which was easy to do in my fragile state. We went to a park outside the city. After I realized the day was over, I told Lorita, "I didn't go." She replied, "I know." She was aware of what had happened. It took me months to reconcile the fact that the people who had been so friendly to me were very manipulative.

Journal entry - I am trying to think of myself as lucky. Lucky to be out of cult and lucky to be alive. Not sure of people, they were all so friendly, all they wanted was my money. Lucky Lorita knew there was something wrong.

I was very drained. The course had messed me up and not fixed anything. I contacted the Cult Information Center and I was told it would just take time for the effects to wear off. The signals for my bodily functions were disrupted. I carried a list with me so that I could narrow down and identify the sensations in my body.

The list had options: eat, drink or go to the bathroom. I could not readily identify the sensations so the list helped me make the connection in my mind. The process was typical for someone who had had a brain-washing experience.

As I was so unsure of myself, I moved in with my mom who was drinking heavily and confined to her bed; she had developed overpowering pain in her legs that she could not convince her doctor to treat. I think she was self-medicating to deal with the excruciating pain. The brain-washing seemed to be of some benefit as it took away the fear of going to university. I would come in from a full day at classes and find nothing in the house had changed. It was very discouraging.

Inside of me was a deep lack of courage and confidence as well as a blank feeling in my brain. I needed help. I accessed the student counselling center for help with my inability to concentrate because of the brainwashing. The counsellor helped me withdraw from the courses I was in, but that created more W's (Withdrawals). I then took more courses which I should have audited but I took them for marks in spite of my difficulties. I couldn't do it. Taking the courses finished off the chance I had been given and the Dean asked me to leave the university again. I appealed. The university was very understanding and said I could continue counselling if it was helping me. I had a different counsellor than the one I had started with; she had developed a stress-related illness and had left the university, so I did not continue counselling. I decided I was a confirmed failure.

Journal entry - I don't know why I even bothered....Nothing is ever going to work out.

I was disappointed, discouraged and at a loss about what to do to help myself.

My friend Wanda* asked me out for a drink but I said "No." "Come on, I'll buy you a drink." I reluctantly agreed. We went to a little bar that reminded Wanda of her home town in Saskatchewan. It was kind of run-down but homey at the same time.

We walked into Cabana Joe's, sat down and ordered. "One dark ale." The waitress brought it quick as wink. We were talking and I was trying not to think about the wrong way my life was going when some guy we didn't know came over to our table, pointed at a dark-haired fellow at another table and said, "That guy over there wants to meet you girls. Can he join you?" We were not opposed to the idea, so we shrugged our shoulders and said "Okay." Then, the same guy went over to the dark-haired fellow's (Wade's) table and said, "Those girls over there want to meet you, so why don't you go over and join them." Wade thought, "Why not, if they want to meet me. I'll just go over and talk to them and see how it goes." Wade came over and sat beside me and introduced himself. I was normally wary of new people, but I immediately trusted him and without my normal courting filters and defenses turned on because of my brainwashing experience, I told him so. We chatted the evening away.

I told Wade I was going to Radium with my family for the weekend and he could call me on Monday if he wanted. I didn't normally give out my phone number but this was different. I was hoping he would call. He did. My family drove home from Radium in two cars. My middle brother was in one car and it arrived first. Wade called. My brother answered the phone. When I arrived ten minutes afterward and emerged from the second car, he gave me the message. I called Wade back the second I found out. "You called!" I exclaimed, not able to contain my excitement. He said, "Of course I called; you thought I wouldn't call you? No girl has ever talked so easily with me. I am really busy going to school and working, but I would like to see you." I wasn't thinking of a permanent relationship because I wasn't sure how long it would take me to recover.

We met for coffee every Tuesday after his work and after a class I was taking on how to care for myself as an adult child of an alcoholic. He was my knight in shining armour. I was so vulnerable after being brainwashed. I was very open to any suggestion and Wade was a great influence. He had a healthy attitude toward life which I adopted, so I was recovering at a steady rate. Wade graduated and we continued dating. After we dated for two years, we moved in together. Then, one Christmas something changed everything.

Wade and I went Christmas shopping and we were trying to figure out where to eat. I thought Wade wasn't feeling well because he was kind of pale. I said, "Let's grab something quick like a hamburger." He replied, "No." Wade named a few of the restaurants we liked to visit and I didn't agree. I made a couple of other suggestions he turned down so I asked, "Why don't we just go home?"

Once in the door, I sat on the bed, Wade knelt down beside me and said the words I thought would never be said to me. "Will you marry me?" he asked. At first, I told him no because I thought things don't always work out for me. Then, right away,

I said, "Yes." I refused to let fear steal the day. I soon realized that Wade was trying to get me to a nice restaurant in order to propose marriage and I hadn't been very cooperative. That night, I phoned my mom and found out she knew because Wade had asked her permission to marry me.

Chapter 4

The Tsunami

We decided to pay for the wedding ourselves. We thought it would take us about two years to save up. My mom phoned one night, and in a very serious tone, asked us to move up the wedding by a year. If we did, she said, she would pay for it. It sounded like a good idea and we agreed.

Everything, it seemed, went wrong. Our minister left before he had the chance to marry us, and the new minister wanted to marry us every time we saw him since marrying us was the last duty he had to do before he retired. My maid of honour became pregnant, so she decided to bow out of her responsibilities. My bridesmaids complained about the dresses even though I specifically picked them for each bridesmaid's figure type and the dresses were teal velvet, so my friends could wear them again to another formal function or on New Year's Eve. Also, the bridesmaids did not get along, in part because they did not know each other because they were from different groups of friends.

There were other disagreements. I knew what I wanted my wedding to be. I wanted a band. Wade wanted a D.J. Wade got his way. I wanted a small wedding at a restaurant in Bragg Creek; my mom wanted a full out wedding with all the relatives. My mom got her way. Then, my mom said I wasn't grateful since she was paying for everything and she had not been included in any of the decisions. At the eleventh hour, she threatened not to pay because she did not feel appreciated. But I was grateful. The day after we decided to get married, I had bought a gift I was going to give to her the day of the wedding. It was so difficult to navigate the politics of the wedding.

Aunts, uncles and cousins from far and wide had come to see us wed. Wade's brother and his family, as well as my brother and his family came from across the country to make it even more memorable. Everything, as far as I knew, was in order for my big day.

September 3rd 1993 dawned brightly. We had planned a beautiful ceremony followed by a sit-down prime rib dinner for 120 guests. There were pearl-coloured balloons in the shape of a heart that sat above the head table where Wade and I were going to eat our first meal together as husband and wife. It mirrored the invitation we had sent out. The theme in my mind was one heart, one lifetime. My dress had been in an advertisement for the wedding shop I bought it from and my mom had a matching veil and purse made for me for my special day. Everything was taken care of, down to the last detail.

I did not sleep the night before the wedding because there were no curtains on the window in my old bedroom at my mom's house and the street lights kept me awake. My contact lens ripped and because of vanity, I did not wear my glasses on my wedding day. Instead, I wore just one contact lens. At the hairdresser's, I realized I forgot my veil and the limo driver had to go back for it. Once we were all ready, all the bridesmaids got in the limo and somebody said, "Everybody's here." The limo driver started driving to the church when I realized my mother and my mother-in-law Elsie were still back at the house with no way to get to the church, so we had to go back to get them.

There were other problems. My family's politics added to the stress of the day – everyone had an opinion and, it seems, an agenda. No one was thinking about how I was feeling. I was having trouble sticking up for what I needed.

The wedding itself went well even though a few things went wrong. We almost did not have food at the wedding. A few days before the event, I had a meltdown in front of the caterer and he misunderstood and thought we weren't getting married because my mom threatened not to pay.

The following day, I dropped off the check with his wife, who did not tell him and we arrived at the event and nothing had been prepared. I was in a room alone while my guests waited in the vestibule. The caterers asked my mom to show them a receipt proving she paid. She was mad. In the end, the caterers did manage to feed everybody. My mom was mad a lot that day: we did not dance as gracefully as she would have liked, and the food was not to her liking – just two of many other things. According to the mother of the bride, it was not perfect and therefore, it was a complete failure – black and white thinking at its best. The day had not gone entirely the way I had envisioned either and I got sucked into perfectionist thinking. Instead of feeling triumphant, a feeling of failure affected the way I felt about myself and the whole affair. I had tried my best to please everybody and no one realized what a fragile state I was in. I needed a vacation.

We flew to Barbados for our honeymoon and we had a restful two weeks free from the worries leading up to the wedding. The island of Barbados was beautiful. We did all the touristy things such as touring a rum plant and seeing gardens and when we ran out of money, we laid on the beach. We had fabulous meals. We ate at an old house converted into a restaurant. It overlooked the ocean and while we ate a gecko came down the coconut tree and sat on the railing and watched us.

We thought this was a start of a fabulous life together.

When we came back from our honeymoon, I was sure some of our wedding gifts were missing. We rented a camera, hid it in the living room and taped day and night hoping to catch whoever was stealing from us. Wade spent hours watching the tapes after he got home from work. I called the police and they said to move out of the apartment where we lived.

Journal entry - I am glad that I called the police. I want my stuff back. I am packing and it is painful to leave under such stressful circumstances. I am relieved that there will be no more wondering when something is going missing. No more feeling like someone's been in my house... It feels like they were trying to wreck our lives. Wade and I almost split up over this. Still no solid proof.

The fear, however, came with me wherever I went. We moved at least 3 more times that year. We only stayed three weeks in one apartment. It was crazy. I was paranoid of going to the laundry room (someone had talked to me while I was there and I vowed never to go in there again, not any laundry room, ever). The laundry piled up and Wade complained about not having clean socks. My answer was to wash them in the sink with dish soap and dry them in the oven where I watched them closely so they would not get too hot and melt. There were other signs that I was not functioning normally.

I was also losing weight from not eating. Wade took me out to eat a lot. I would pick at my food and then throw the take-home leftovers out the next day while Wade was at work. When we did buy groceries they were soon gone. Wade thought I might have an eating disorder because I was so thin and the groceries were obviously disappearing. He was bringing the groceries in the front door and I was throwing them out the back door because I thought my food was poisoned. My new husband said to one of his friends: "My wife rocks! She takes out her own garbage!" Little did he know that this meant trouble.

I also thought my possessions were being stolen so I would hide the items that were important to me. I thought my hairbrush had been stolen and I complained to Wade. He looked and looked and finally found my brush between the mattress and the box spring. He confronted me, "Is this what you are looking for?" I did not remember until that moment that I had hidden my brush so no one would take it. We fought about something every day.

Finally, my mom thought we should buy a house and then no one but us would have a key. This strategy did not work. I bought security bars for the doors and windows and still could not leave the house in case someone came in and poisoned my food or took something. I would be in the house and then retreat to my bedroom and then to my bed. Someone would find out we were recently married and say something like "Oh, so the honeymoon is not over yet." Wade thought to himself, "Two weeks – I had only two weeks of happiness."

Wade suspected I was suicidal, so he asked me if I was, and I replied, "Yes." He asked, "You think people are bothering you, don't you?" Again, I said, "Yes." He asked me another question: "Why don't you hang around and piss them all off?" It was the exact right thing to say to me. I got righteously indignant and thought, "I am not killing myself and they can't make me."

I was desperate for the problems to end because I was not going out. I wasn't driving. I wasn't making dinner. I was not having fun. I thought people were watching me and monitoring me so I could not do anything. I did not phone my friends. I talked to my mom on the phone sometimes but I thought someone was listening to my conversations with her. She was my only outside contact. I did not have the normal life of a young bride.

My breaking point came. Wade and I had another fight and I remember getting down on my knees and praying. I felt forsaken – I felt abandoned by God. I confessed my regret for everything I could think of. I poured out my heart. I did not feel anything but I thought it would probably take twenty years for this to work out. I did not get my answer right away which made me think, "God isn't listening."

I just carried on my way, living a lonely, miserable life, not having any idea that the problem was within me, like everyone else was telling me. "They are wrong – they don't see what I see," I thought. I did not realize I was risking my marriage because of my decisions not to listen to other people. I kept asking, "Why have I lost my credibility? Why don't you believe me?" I was teetering on belligerent when anyone brought up the idea that I should go see a doctor. My friend Lorita's mom asked, "What in the world has gotten into Elizabeth?"

Journal entry - Paranoid jumpy think the downside content think the upside confident progressing despair downcast lethargic not wanting to act procrastination unhealthy worried miffed not sure why this is happening to me powerless empty

I wasn't sleeping very well and I got up in the middle of the night to watch for suspicious-looking cars. I stayed in the house night and day. Leaving the house was the thieves' only opportunity to get in without my vigilance stopping them; it was not worth the risk. As well, I stopped showering. When I showered, I was too preoccupied to watch the door and it became the only time that things could go missing. It made perfect sense to me. I had been on my guard for almost two years. I did not have very many friends left – except for Deanna.

I reconnected with Deanna in August 1995. I hadn't seen Deanna for years. We met when we were seven. Although she moved away, for years, we spent the summers together no matter where she lived. Eventually I lost touch with her. We hadn't seen each other for about a decade. She missed my wedding because I did not have an address to send her an invitation. One day, she phoned my mom, who still had the same phone number I had when I was growing up. She got my phone number and directions to my house and came over for a visit.

She and I had a long visit. "Can I stay and meet Wade? I would really like to meet him." She waited four hours until he came home from work. She distracted me with a task in the living room and spoke with Wade in the kitchen. "Elizabeth, I believe, is in psychosis. This isn't going to get better on its own. You have to take her to the hospital where she can get assessed. You must do it as soon as possible." Wade's denial was broken. The new bride jitters were worse than he imagined. He did what any sane person would do – the next day he took me on a date.

Wade thought up a date that would be irresistible for me so I would be more likely to say yes to leaving the house. We used to go to the ice cream kiosk near Bowens* Park and drive around the lagoon until our ice cream had disappeared into our tummies. It was something my Dad and I used to do when I was a young girl. Wade asked me if I wanted to go for ice cream like we used to. I was reluctant but it seemed important to him so I relented. We got our ice cream and then drove around the park. I did not enjoy it as I had in the past. I was looking at the other cars and thought maybe we were being followed. On the drive home, Wade made a detour.

We drove up the small hill to the hospital and I realized where I was. I was furious. I got out of the car and tried to run away. Wade ran after me and caught me. Then, Wade said what I thought made sense. He said, "Go in there and tell the doctors what has been happening to you and if they think we should call the police that is what we will do." I thought, "I'll go in there and tell the doctors what has been done to me and they will see we need to call the police. Bring it on." I went willingly.

Chapter 5

Shelter from the Storm

Once past emergency triage, people see a steady stream of professionals. First, someone sees a student nurse, then a nurse, then a resident doctor, then a doctor, then a resident psychiatrist, then a psychiatrist. For me, the process, I think, took 17 hours. I remember the nurse giving me a sandwich which I threw away because I thought it might be poisoned and the nurse told my husband, "There is something really wrong with your wife." It made me not trust the medical staff, but I decided I had to if this was going to get resolved. I told them exactly what was going on, expecting them to call the police. I was admitted, I was out of tears, and my intuition was overtaxed. My adrenaline was depleted because of living for two years in a fight or flight response. I did not have the energy to fight the decision.

Journal entry - staying on the psychiatric ward is institutional living. The meals are brought up in tray towers and at a specific time I go and get the tray that has my name on it. There are programs during the week where we make key chains or bake. It is therapeutic, I guess. Not pleasant.

From 5-9 pm I looked forward to visitors. Wade came every night after work. I told him that there were people living in the dugout in our lawn and they were getting in the house through an opening hidden hidden behind the dartboard in the basement. I made him promise that he would make sure they weren't getting in, that maybe he could plug the hole. He nodded and promised he would check it out.

Sometimes, my youngest brother drove my mom to the hospital to see me. My mother would ask me if I needed anything: every time I said "bigger underwear." I was gaining weight very rapidly on my new medication (a common side effect). It probably didn't help that I had screwed up my metabolism from not eating and now I was eating very well because I thought the food was safe. I went from a size 8 to a size 14 in six weeks. This change was bad enough from a health standpoint, but it also had psychological ramifications. Not only did I not feel like myself, I did not look like myself.

Weeks crept by with my multiple conspiracy theories explained on numerous occasions to doctors who did not say too much but just wrote notes on what I was saying. I felt like I was on a slow train to nowhere. Finally, I asked the doctor what was wrong with me. He said "I think you have schizophrenia." The doctor sent me home with a card for counselling and prescriptions for anti-psychotic medication. So much for my ornate theories.

People asked me if it was a relief getting a diagnosis, and for me it wasn't. I really couldn't believe that I was not right, that my perception could be so far off. My mind tricked me and it was a blow to my self-esteem. The problem with schizophrenia is that I couldn't trust my senses. I grew up trusting my sense of touch, taste, hearing, seeing, and smell. My self-esteem plummeted when I found out my senses had lied to me. It was very disconcerting.

Chapter 6

After the Waters Recede

Upon smelling a mixture of dark roast coffee and bacon I woke up the first day out of hospital and realized I was in my own bed. A comforting luxury. Wade came into the bedroom and said, "Oh, you are awake! Why don't you get dressed and come down for breakfast? I am making you pancakes." I had slipped into a haughty, self-pity mood and replied, "I am not getting dressed – I am sick!"

An expression I had never seen came over Wade's face. He was serious but there was a hint of anger. He retorted, "My wife is going to get dressed and meet me downstairs for breakfast in 10 minutes." And he turned on his heel and marched out the door, back to the kitchen. I was stunned;

he had never spoken to me like that before. I thought, "What if he is serious? I want to be his wife. Maybe I should get dressed?" It shocked me into sense and set the tone for my recovery. Sorrow is acceptable; self-pity is not. I got dressed, went down for breakfast and started on the journey towards being mentally healthy.

Being mentally healthy included a goal group. I had been in a goal setting group while in hospital. We each set three goals a day. At first, the goals were things like make my bed, take a shower and phone my mom which were huge goals to me at the time. I stayed in the goal group as an outpatient for eight months. Every day, I set goals and got my checkmarks. If I was having trouble getting a goal, I would ask the group to help me brainstorm; if I was having trouble reaching a goal, Kathleen, the group leader and occupational therapist, would ask if the goal was one I really wanted. My goals got bigger: try to save my marriage; find the schizophrenia society; and find a job.

Journal entry - The more of life you master the less of life you fear. All problems notwithstanding I am fine. I am learning to set goals and making progress. No one seems to see my faults here in goal group. I have several problems. Kathleen said just start somewhere and then overcome the obstacles one at a time. It is scary to realize you don't have the problem you thought you had but you have a lot of problems you did not know you had.

Chapter 7

Trying to Rebuild

My marriage was in shambles for obvious reasons. I realized part of our marriage difficulties were because I had not given Wade any emotional support for the first two years of our marriage. I made Wade a goal. I wanted to let him know I loved him, so I did three nice things for him a day: notes in his socks; banana bread for his coffee break; clean socks; a phone call to encourage him at work, etc. Lots of little, doable things. I told Wade not to acknowledge me for these things but to just know that I loved him. Things started to improve.

Wade came to me after a couple of months and told me, "I am not sure yet if I am staying with you, but I won't leave you until I think you are strong enough to be on your own."

Journal entry -

Alone? Together?

Which will be my fate?

My soul mate first rate

Not to be are our dreams that once we

Dreamed for,

Worked for,

Lived with,

He is capital "D"

Disappointed

Oh my God Oh my God Oh my God

Answer my prayer for a different life

One filled with Joy, Hope, Life.

I am sorry my love,

So sorry,

I am sick

We went to counselling and the social worker said we should take turns planning dates. These dates only accentuated the pain. We would be together on our date and struggle to talk about even the most mundane topics. We spent most of our time in complete silence.

We quit counselling and decided to not talk about how things were going. I still did three nice things for him a day. I told Wade I was not going to ask him what he was thinking, that we would have a cup of tea every night like we used to when we were dating and start from there. No talk except for practical, "What are you doing tomorrow?" We weren't even eating dinner together, since I did not have the skills to organize a meal and he was burying himself in his work and coming home late.

It didn't help that I had halved my pills. I felt I really wasn't as sick as I had been; therefore, I thought that I would be better off if I was on a lower dose. I was desperate not to be so sick. I was sitting on the couch, and I heard this loud, mean, booming voice: "You better clean up this house or your husband will never come home!" I started to cry and realized that I might have something after all. I ended up in the hospital. This time it was shorter and I came out much wiser.

Unbeknownst to me my mother called Wade. "If you want to leave Elizabeth we understand. You haven't been married that long and maybe you should get on with your own life." He replied, "No, I made a vow to Elizabeth and I am going to do my best to honour that promise."

Journal entry - March 1995. Still tired after sleeping 18 hours a day I am going to goal group, waiting up for Wade until he gets home around 8 o'clock and then bed. All I can do. Kathleen said to phone Schizophrenia Society. I will do it Monday for sure.

I phoned the Schizophrenia Society office and an enthusiastic practicum student answered. He convinced me to stay on the line until someone named Mary* could talk to me. Her voice was very warm: "I know you're probably busy, but I was wondering if you couldn't come and down and help

me pick out snacks for the meeting." Being
the helpful sort, I drove downtown, very
determined to help out in this very important mission.

I met Fay that day and this turned out
to be the beginning of a very important
chapter in my life. That day I found a purpose to my suffering – to end the stigma
of mental illness by educating people. It
was Fay's passion that got me excited. She
was Partnership Education Coordinator
at the Schizophrenia Society. She believes
the stigma surrounding someone with the
mental illness is as bad as the illness itself.
Her vision was to change people's perception of what mental illness really is. Fay
coached me and I started speaking about
my illness for the Partnership Program.

In the summer of 1998, at a picnic
put on by another mental health agency,
a theatre company performed a play written for the agency. We, the members of
the Partnership Program, got the name
of the theatre company and told Fay. She
contacted the theatre group and our Part-

nership Program members were asked to help write a play. Over the summer, using our experiences as the subject matter, we work-shopped the play and came up with a great script. *Starry Starry Night* was supposed to be a one-time only performance and I played the female lead. However, it was in so much demand that it is still being performed fifteen years later. It is reader's theatre so no one has to memorize lines. The parts are fluid so participants can start with a non-speaking role and then the next time have a few lines and then have bigger roles as they get more comfortable with the performance aspect.

The next goal I wanted to accomplish was to find a part-time job. I handed in my resume to an employment agency that helped people with disabilities find jobs. The agency found me a job doing speeches for the City of Calgary in the disability awareness program. It was fun. Fay and I made up a game about schizophrenia called the brain game which I led after telling my story. I worked there for five years.

I worked with a woman, Donna*, and she spoke to students about living with cerebral palsy; she had a facilitator named Anna* help her with the logistics of having a job. We were all friends and one day after a speech Anna said that I might be a good fit for working with people with her agency. I applied and was accepted and it was the most educational, supportive experience I could have asked for.

The staff of the Progressive Alternatives Society of Calgary (PASC) is progressive in their attitudes toward people with disabilities. Disability is taken as a fact of life. People are asked, "What do you want to do with your life?"

As a community facilitator, I tried to help the person answer the question and make it happen. The process had an unexpected benefit for me. As I learned Dr. Wolfensberger's theory (that PASC's work was based on) I applied it to my own course of disability and gained an understanding of how to overcome the stigma associated with a mental illness.

The people running the agency were understanding of my disability as well. Early on in my career at PASC I called my boss.

"I am afraid of the rain so I can't go out."

"Call me tomorrow after you get some rest," she replied.

I phoned the next day.

"I am still feeling crummy."

She responded, "Well, take care and give me a call tomorrow in the morning."

I called on day three and had a meltdown.

"I can't do this job," I cried. "Maybe it was a mistake to hire me. I am letting everyone down."

My boss replied, "What? No one has the flu for three days ever? Call me when you feel better."

It was the kindest thing to do for me at that point. I think about what would have happened if I had any other boss. Maybe they would have said, "You are right. It was a mistake to hire you. Consider yourself fired." I am lucky this was not the case.

PASC practises what it preaches. I was accepted and there were accommodations along the way if I wasn't feeling well. My subsequent bosses, Nicole and her boss Bill (Executive Director), always supported me and appreciated my hard work. It is part of the PASC philosophy that people are valuable in spite of any disability. The work I did there was valued. I was valued. I came to view myself as valuable.

Journal entry - I can't believe that I have job that has: ongoing training, enough money, a higher purpose all the things that I wrote down that I wanted in a job. I am very valued as an employee at PASC because the supervisors know I have a clear idea of what it is like to be devalued and how important it is to help someone do all they can to minimize the effects. I love my job.

Chapter 8

Grey Cloudy Days

I had a bit of money, and found myself with a bit of extra energy so I decided to throw Wade a surprise party. He was turning thirty. I didn't make a guest list. I just phoned people from his address book and told his co-workers to spread the word. I was not a very experienced party planner, so I did not write anything down. That way he would not find out by accident. I was so excited and worked up about the party. We had 30 flamingos coming for the lawn (I was splitting the cost with my mom) and it was going to be great. I thought I would shop for food and liquor the day of the party, so Wade would have no idea. He was going to be so surprised!

Everything was going well the day before the party, until I started to clean up. I was kind of running around like a chicken with my head cut off, not sure where to start. To begin, I decided to clean half of the living room. Before I knew it, I slipped into a psychotic state and remember having a hallucination that my head had exploded right off my shoulders. I continued to clean with an imaginary line dividing the living room. I cleaned half of the coffee table and half of the sofa, until there was a clear definite dividing line of messy side and clean side diagonally across the room. I also cleaned out all my nicer clothes and put them in garbage bags, so the garbage men could come and pick them up to take them to my other reality. Both Wade and I were going there after the party. This did not seem like an unreasonable set of thoughts.

The ringing phone interrupted me. Fay called and said, "I'll pick you up if you want to come over for a visit." It was clear to her that I was having trouble and she phoned my mom, who phoned my brother, to pick me up and take me to the hospital. I was mad because Fay wrote a note to the psychiatrist who would see me. I asked Fay, "Who told you I am hearing voices?" I did not think I was. I ended up in hospital.

My mom phoned Wade at work: "Elizabeth has been admitted. By the way, you are having a party tomorrow night; it was supposed to be a surprise. I don't think she had a list of who was invited, in case you found it. It is up to you, if you want to turn people away at the door. I don't see any other option."

Wade came home to half a clean house. He had to keep it together and make the party happen. Why did he not just cancel it? After all, I was in the hospital. The answer was stigma. Not everyone knew I had the diagnosis. In order to say I was in the hospital he would have to answer the next question: "What's wrong with her?" He did not want to deal with that, especially with people he worked with who did not know. (They probably did, but did not let on). In addition, he did not know who I had contacted to retract the invitation. Instead, he dodged questions about my whereabouts all night. Sixty people with sixty questions were told, "Her mom is sick, so she had to go help her."

I missed the party and the flamingos. In fact, it was all over by the time I came to my senses a couple of days later. My clothes had been taken away by the garbage men never to be seen again. It was so humiliating.

Journal entry - The stigma is still there but I am going to be open about my diagnosis now. If it is a deal breaker for a friendship developing I would rather know that in advance. All my friends and family know and that is the way I want it. No secrets. No unexpected surprises.

Chapter 9

Ray of Sunshine

Being open about my illness was one of the things Arlo, my counsellor, taught me after this last hospitalization. I didn't consciously know all of what he taught me but I incorporated these thoughts into my wellness:

- Accept what is and then you will be able to assess what to do next.

- Don't worry about what people think of you. They probably are not thinking of you at all. Don't let other people determine how you feel about yourself.

- Today is enough trouble without all the fear and worry of all the tomorrows piled on top of it. Worry about today and plan a bit for tomorrow and once a moment is over move on to the next moment. Regret long enough to learn the lesson and then let it go.

- Someone will always have negative comments, so don't let them bother you. They are coming from their own perspective and have their own ideas about how they want the world to be. Your perspective is just as valid.

- Do not base your needs on other's ability to meet your needs. Identify your needs and be creative about getting them met. Do not rely on one person to meet your needs. Your needs are important – take care of yourself and be gentle with yourself.

- All emotions are fine as long as you express them in a healthy way. Do not blame the other person for the way you feel. You must take responsibility for the way you are feeling and know only you have the power to change you and, therefore, the situation.

- Go back to university. It is unfinished business.

Journal entry - I applied to get in with a letter of support from Arlo and the university agreed I could take classes. Arlo said to not worry about graduating but just take one course to try it out for the therapeutic value. My mom is paying for my course. Mom bought me a leather coat that I will use as my suit of armour to protect me from the scariness of this return to school. I am cautiously optimistic.

Top: Just before my first hospitalization, 1995. I had just cut my own hair short.
Left: Dad (Jack Dunbar), 1986.

Mom, University of Calgary, Bachelor of Education 1972.

Top: Wade and I on our wedding day, 1993.
Bottom (Left to Right): Fay, mom and I.

Elizabeth, University of Calgary, Bachelor of
Communication and Culture 2010.

Chapter 10

Every Cloud
Has a Silver Lining

University 3.0

I registered for winter semester in January of 2000. I only took one course the first year. Sociology was my first choice. I sat beside a young law student who took me under his wing and allayed my fears about my abilities. He lent me his notes and to my surprise they were almost identical to what I had written down. He helped me set up my library card and told me all the other things I needed to know. The Disability Resource Centre Director on campus suggested I aim for B's. B is a respectable mark and does not require the extra pressure of being perfect. I got a B on my first course;

I was on my way. Around this time Wade fell back in love with me. I think he could see how hard I was trying.

I began to tackle other parts of my life also. My disorganized mind was reflected in my disorganized space so a friend and an organizer, Barb, helped me organize our house and make it home. It was something I could not do without help. Barb patiently went through my things with me and taught me how to organize them. At times, I would be overwhelmed by the emotions behind what had happened to me, which were made apparent by the items or what they represented to me. Barb helped me take it a step at a time. It was a very healing process. Barb organized things in a way that made sense to me and all I really did was decide what to keep or throw away. It made a big difference in our lifestyle.

From my in-laws, Dave and Elsie, who were living with us for the winter while waiting to buy a house in Alberta, I learned to make dinner. They let me watch in the kitchen and were my advice givers when I had questions about how to proceed when I started making dinner without them there to guide me; they were just a phone call away.

Journal entry - My priorities continue to be school, Wade, speaking, making a decent dinner, going to Bible study, keeping the house well, and keeping the relationship with my mom. All areas were going well, even though mom and I are still not consistently getting along. It is frustrating. This was the only way it will ever be, I guess.

I continued taking courses at the university and during one winter semester my mom landed in the hospital. I was unaware of what was in store. My mom slipped into a coma. My faith was at an all time low and was disappearing fast. With each passing day my mother was starving to death. She was 97 pounds – just skin and bones – not responding. She had been like this for 12 days and on day 11, the doctors had stopped feeding her. I stopped doing everything too, except for the bare essentials. No

Bible study, just work and school. Louise, my Bible study table leader, noticed and she phoned me.

"Elizabeth, you have stopped coming on Tuesdays. We miss you."

"I can't come. My mom is in the hospital in a coma. She is going to die. I am trying to work and go to school. I can't do everything. Besides, I'm not sure I believe in God anyhow."

"Sounds serious. Do you mind if I come to the hospital and pray with you?"

"If you want to," I said trying to hide the fact that I did not believe anything would help, especially prayer.

"I'll come tomorrow," she said.

I was surprised when she showed up at the hospital.

We prayed by my mom's bedside and she finished the prayer by saying, "Frances, I want you to sit up and talk to Elizabeth the next time you see her, God willing. Amen."

At my next visit, my mom sat up and asked, "Can I have a pop?" "You don't like pop?!" I replied. I was shocked because my mother sat up and spoke to me after lying motionless for a week and a half. I was stunned because she had never asked for a pop in her life!

"Okay then, how about a milk?" I went to the nurses' station to enquire about a glass of milk and a team of nurses came rushing into the room. In the days following, there were medical professionals streaming through her room wanting to meet the woman who woke up from a coma after 12 days.

I phoned Louise to tell her the good news, and she said to ask my mom if she wanted to accept Jesus. I asked and my mom nodded. I told her, "Ask Jesus to come and live with you in your heart and to forgive you for your sins." She did just that.

Journal Entry - My biggest worry was that my mom will die before we have had a chance to resolve our conflict. She is paying for my university and is supportive, but there is still an uncomfortable cavern between us. God, it seemed, has answered my secret prayer; both she and I have another chance to fix our broken relationship. I realized God is for me, and He is there to help me with whatever I face. Real Faith Established.

There came a point soon after, when all my mother wanted was peace with her children. I felt, in a way, that she had matured out of the pity-party mode. My mother was on morphine for the pain in her legs and she was not drinking anymore. She and I got along very well at times, in some respects, better than we ever had.

She and I would go on shopping escapades. I would put her wheelchair in the trunk of the car and we would just go for a look. Then, we would buy clothes to wear. My mom told me, "I can't make you feel good, necessarily, but I can make sure you look good." We had such fun. We would go to the hamburger counter at the department store where the waitress, Val, knew us by name. We always had a hamburger with fries. We always threatened that we would come for dessert only and one day we finally did. We decided to spoil our dinners and just have dessert. There was something deliciously defiant about eating dessert instead of dinner, especially when out with mom. Our plan was flawless, except the diner had run out of dessert save for one lonely piece of cherry pie. My mom ate it but we laughed at the irony that we had come to the diner and had entertained the idea of only having dessert for dinner many times and when we decided to do it there was no dessert to be had!

School was going swimmingly. One morning, after class, I was asked by one of my professors to do an independent study. Dr. Charles* wanted me to do a project of my choosing. I felt smart. Someone else, a professor, had noticed that I was smart.

A fear of success came upon me with a vengeance; my old habit of sabotaging myself kicked in and I got writer's block. I would talk with my professor about the project but could not write a thing. I had a single page after one semester. He said, "Let's just forget it." Then, I realized there had been a misunderstanding about the registration.

Journal entry - Oh my God I have wasted an entire semester. I was not registered. I misunderstood and thought it was special registration and the professor did it. Wasted time and energy. I have to try to stop thinking about all that, because we were spending Christmas with Wade's mom and Dad.

Bright and early on the day before Christmas Eve, we picked up a crown of pork and started on our journey to see Wade's parents in Trochu. I had been having a string of bad days in terms of the illness resulting in a meltdown. It is hard because at times I felt so ashamed of the illness and I thought I should leave Wade so he could have a carefree life. "Maybe this is a big mistake," I told him, "and we should go our separate ways so you won't have to worry about me anymore." "You think that I won't worry about you any-way?" he replied. "I would worry about you no matter what, whether you're with me in the same house or not. It would be easier for me if we lived in the same house, so why don't we to stay together? We're OK. You are OK. You've just had a couple of bad days. It's the end of the semester and this is the stress of Christmas. Why don't we talk about it later when you're not so stressed out?" The voice of reason won out. The illness was our only problem; we had worked everything else out. We drove for an hour and a half and talked about how far we had come and how we always managed to have a good Christmas every year.

Wade's dad, Dave, was a British trained chef and we knew we were in for a treat. We arrived at noon and ate a fabulous lunch in the 100-year-old A-frame house that used to be the doctor's house in town. Dave and Elsie, the cutest couple, had been married almost 50 years.

On Christmas Eve, we had "pickies" for dinner: crab tarts, salmon tarts, pickles and cheese with some Christmas cheer in the form of hot chocolate.

Christmas morning we were up at 5:30. Mom, Elsie, stirred her tea so loudly and for so long that it was not a mistake that we were awake. We opened presents. Fun. For Christmas dinner we had the stuffed roast crown of pork and pumpkin pie for dessert. Mom made some lemon tarts and almond tarts. It was very festive.

The next day we had English lunch: pickled walnuts, onions, ham and crusty rolls, and very English brown saucy pickles. It seems all we did was eat! If someone left the Andersons hungry it was their own fault. Wade's mom told him to have some more, that he looked hungry. He replied, "I am not hungry and if I keep eating like this I'll never fit into my pants." We laughed because Wade would never be fat and Elise said in a funny voice with her sweet English accent, "Not your problem, Dear." It was nice to rest and forget all the worries of city life. We had a fabulous visit and we were renewed for the coming New Year.

After Christmas, I returned to school determined to succeed. I wanted the opportunity to do an independent study more than anything, so I registered and changed projects. I was going to analyze my own journal. Easy? No. I made categories, cut and pasted, and then did not know how to put it into any kind of format that made sense. I read books. I thought. I could not write. The semester went by quickly and with only three weeks left Dr. Charles advised me to take a "W" because no one can write a decent twenty plus page paper in three weeks. It was better than an "F," he explained.

I had failed. I was dejected. I was told to go see the Dean to get my "W." I was afraid because I had such a bad record from before. The Dean explained, "You don't have to see me. You should see the Associate Dean (who was in another building)." Trying to lighten the mood, the Dean told me he had the power as he changed my mark on the computer. He was very understanding and assured me that it would not affect my standing since I had done so well this third time in university except for this one blip.

As I was sitting by the elevators, wondering how I was going to finish this work, I ran into one of my former professors, Dr. Margo Husby. I was dressed up and she asked, "What are you doing here?" I told her how I had tried to analyze my journal and I was going to try to do it on my own, since I had taken a "W" on the course. She told me, "Do it under me. Go back in the Dean's office and tell him you want a spring course to finish what you have started. We will get permission for what you have already done." Not wanting to face the Dean on my own, I said, "You come with me." We marched right past the administrative staff and Dr. Margo spoke to the Dean. "Elizabeth is going to finish what she started with me. General Studies 501, spring semester." We got the paperwork organized. I was going to go for it. It turns out that I had been told to go to the wrong building for the right reason.

Under Dr. Margo's tutelage, I wrote and handed in writing every week. I realized that my mom was an important topic in my journal and Dr. Margo thought I should concentrate on that. My favourite definition for education was to bring out what I already know. This is how I felt about the course which turned out to be an exercise in hermeneutics. I read <u>My Mother, My Self</u> by Nancy Friday and analyzed the text as I processed my mother/daughter relationship. As usual, I was having trouble finishing this paper and it was really bothering me. I told Dr. Margo and she suggested, "Research fear of success and see if that helps." That was the key. Fear of success for a daughter is tied to her relationship to her mother. I was shocked and amazed at what I was learning because as I was processing the information, it was becoming easier to write. While I was visiting my mom in the hospital, I shared a synopsis of my writing with her:

> All anyone wants to be is a fully developed 'I'. 'I' is for independence. It means I am ready to

stand on my own two feet. My developmental imperative is to keep separating from my mom. Before I left home, my mom started to really need my emotional support when I really needed to start being my own person. It was confusing for both of us. According to Friday, I have to recognize that I am my own person in order to love my mother in a healthy way.[2] My capacity to love my mother has increased since I feel I am a stronger 'I'. To say that my separation is complete is not true.[3] The idea that you never stop separating from your mom is thrilling to me because I know the progress I have made is adequate. Not being able to separate is the crux of the matter relating to fear of success. As Friday points out, I realized the letting go of me is up to my mom, the actual going is up to me.[4]

After I explained what I was learning she was so gracious to me. We discussed my new confidence and she told me, "You are coming into your own."

During the year of the independent study, I was doing my best to understand why I kept withdrawing. I thought I was not affected by my mom's alcoholism but I am an expert at withdrawing. It is the same experience as an alcoholic but with no alcohol. I had been plagued with a paralysis of will and overwhelmed since I left home. I think it was at least part of the reason I had not made it to class in my early attempts at university. Doing nothing comes in the form of withdrawing. This was modeled to me by my mother. When stressed out, she would just go to bed and escape from the world. Withdrawal was the way I coped. I would sit on the couch and literally do nothing. Social withdrawal is a symptom of my illness as well. When I was working on my paper, I was in my final steps of recovery from withdrawing. I was fighting the fear of success and the urge to do nothing and then fail. I was winning over the compulsion to withdraw even though I was under quite a bit of stress.

The recovery program leaders who helped me realize that I was withdrawing suggested I take responsibility for my part in any conflict that had occurred and make amends.

Journal entry - I decided to make amends to mom. In the process of writing the paper, I remembered why my mom drank and it makes sense to me because I am in my forties, trying to succeed in the world of academia. I have compassion for her. I have stopped blaming her for being miserable. She had been thwarted and no one had even acknowledged it. I made another visit to her in the hospital, today. We talked about all the historical events. I told her that I understood why she started drinking. I said, "I forgive you for drinking and all the hurt." I confessed that I was sorry for my leaving home and being so distant at times. I sat on the edge of her bed in her hospital room and we both cried. She said specifically, "I give you full permission to succeed." I have new courage.

I wrote the following in my paper:

> My separation from my mother is the never ending process of me becoming myself. Separate but connected – an adult. I have created a list of what it means for me to consider myself an adult. An adult Elizabeth is married, spontaneous, loving, responsible, disciplined (a disciple), an ambassadoer (misspelling intentional), strong, takes time for self-care, smart, educated, on time, good at making dinner, happy. She has a clean room (at least that is the goal), doesn't know everything, knows her needs and is creative about getting them met, has strong relationships, has money, likes her job, keeps her word, has forgiven her parents, makes realistic plans, checks her e-mail, prays and believes in God, feels empow-

ered to make decisions, does what she doesn't want to do to get the result that I want (like making myself write this paper to finish the course and complete this independent study course and ultimately graduate from university).

There is love and connectedness; there is separation and selfhood.

I saw a mother who is more than the idea of mother, rather a human with good attributes and flaws. Accepting my mother as an imperfect being meant accepting myself.

I wrote about my conversation with my mom in my paper along with all the things that I had learned. The course was only six weeks long and I managed to write a 25-page paper about my mom and my "I". I handed it in knowing everything had been resolved – for me and for her. Dr. Margo gave me an "A" on the paper and on the course.

My mom was proud I had completed my paper because she knew how hard-fought my success had been. She was released from hospital and I was relieved that we still had more time.

Chapter 11

The Sun Comes Out

In August 2009, Mom went back to the nursing home and I phoned to say I was coming over. She was in pretty good spirits. As I was coming into the nursing home, I was asked by Angie*, the nurse, to give mom a sponge bath. "I don't know how," I said. "Your mom has asked me to ask you."

It was a significant event and a proclamation of her wanting to be close. I remembered how she had sponge bathed me during the aftermath of my suicide attempt in order to keep my soaring temperature down. She would finish bathing me and then start again: back, front, legs, and arms. She did this all night long while I was in emergency waiting for a bed. Lucky for me, she had been in nurses' training before she met my Dad. I felt my heart warm and I said I would do it and Angie replied she would help. Angie got all the basins and cloths and towels ready for me. Then, she drew the curtain and left us alone. My mom was eighty-five and she was a little slip of a thing. All I could think was she was so tiny. I was aware of how fragile she was. We talked as I sponged her down, and then dried each limb and then put baby powder on her skin. All the tumblers that unlocked the love had lined up. She loved me and needed me and wanted to be close.

Our roles were reversed. We talked about the fact she had very nice, long nails and that I had not been lucky enough to inherit that trait. We laughed that chocolate should actually be a vitamin because she felt better if she had some every day. I thanked her for being my mom. She thanked me for being her daughter. By the time I was finished, we were both completely content. Our relationship was healed and there was no scar.

We had been working on our relationship for almost my entire life – from the age of 15 to 45, almost thirty years. Doing the dance, I called it. She would come forward and I would retreat and then I would come forward and she would step back. Then, over time, we both grew up.

The nurse, Angie, dressed Mom and I took her out to the patio, which was in the courtyard of the nursing home. I got us both a coffee. After sitting in the shade and chatting the afternoon away, we said our farewells knowing that we had shared an important day.

My mom was admitted into the hospital five weeks after I handed in my paper. I saw her just after her admission and the doctors were trying to figure out why she had been dizzy and had passed out. She had been in the hospital a week when Wade took me up to see her again. I entered her hospital room with a feeling of peace and calm and abiding love within me. She couldn't respond to me because she had slipped into a coma. I visited her just by being with her.

I gazed at her face and said "See you later" when I was leaving. I am not sure, but I think I saw her smile.

Journal entry August 8, 2009 - My Mom died today. Wade and I went shopping for her to get her a new outfit in case she woke up. The youngest of my brothers called Wade on his cell so that Wade could tell me. She did not pull through this time. Not this time. Even still, I am at peace. Perfect peace.

Chapter 12

Touching the Rainbow

My relationship with my mom has come full circle. I did not know why she drank until I took the independent study course and did a hermeneutic paper about my relationship with her. Upon completion of the course, I had a sense of coherence and peace I had never experienced before. When my mom died six weeks after I handed in my paper, I was able to face it with courage, knowing there was nothing left unresolved. My relationship issues with my mom were not the result of symptoms of schizophrenia, but solving the conflict released a great deal of emotional stress which has made my symptoms decrease in severity.

My mom was always pleased I chose to speak to educate audiences. We use a team approach in the Partnership Program. A person with the illness and a family member (unrelated) speak as team partners. It is an effective tool in the fight against the stigma of mental illness. I am part of a great team of speakers and we are paid for our expertise.

The members of Partnership Program decided to write a play to share our valuable experiences. Doing the play was a good stepping stone for me. I used the play as an example of how I was getting better. Before the diagnosis and finding Fay, I would introduce myself to people and then proceed to tell them I failed at university. Now, in my Partnership Presentations, I explain that I taught about schizophrenia and acted in the play.

In the past, I wanted to be a drama teacher. Acting in the play is close enough. I have the pieces of my dream even though I will never have it the way I dreamed. (I no longer do the play except on the rare occasion when not enough actors are available. Performing did so much for me, making me want to give other people a chance).

Speaking for the Partnership Program led to my job with the city doing speeches. I worked for the City of Calgary for 5 years. It was great educating the grade six kids. I did 3-5 speeches a week with the summers off. Over time, I changed and I got my strength back. In the beginning, on the evaluations, children would write, "We feel badly for Elizabeth and hope she feels better soon;" toward the end of the five years the children wrote, "There doesn't look like there is anything wrong with Elizabeth."

After my job at the City, I worked for PASC and at the same time I went to university and started to take classes toward a degree. I finished my Bachelor of Communications and Culture in 2010. With the same student number since my original enrolment in 1985, I received a three year degree. It took me twenty-five years to complete a three year degree. The accommodating university policy that allowed my return, along with the support of the people at the Disability Resource Centre, and an understanding workplace, made it possible. And my perseverance paid off.

Wade chose to stay with me, even though it has been tough at times. He has been my sounding board, my pill monitor, my reason to be well, and the love of my life. He is the strongest, most compassionate person I have ever known. He has been there for me every step of the way and continues to be.

My Recipe for Success

Being mentally healthy while having a mental illness requires six ingredients: timely intervention; the right medications; supportive people (especially loved ones); a reason to be well; a reason to hope; something important to do or a higher purpose or calling.

Timely Intervention

The catalyst to my wellness was Deanna's and then Wade's intervention. Intervention is key since often there is a lack of insight because the part of the brain that would make a person aware is broken. If I don't think I am sick, I am not going to go to the doctor to get treatment. I was in this frame of mind before Deanna and Wade intervened. I did not realize I needed help until after I was admitted to hospital. I am well because I had help accessing medical services. After an intervention, there must be a decision to accept and work with the illness while basing future decisions on what is best now that a new reality, which includes an illness, exists.

The Right Medication

My psychiatrist figured out the medication. Medication is essential to correcting the imbalance in the brain. There should be no shame in taking medication for a mental illness. Why is it any different than taking an aspirin for a headache or insulin for diabetes? The brain needs a corrective measure and the medication provides the correction – it is medication for an imbalance.

The medication mix is a conundrum. Doctors do their best to find the right medication. Finding the right medication is achieved through trial and error, which can create frustration for the patient and the doctor. Even then, the medication can stop working for no apparent reason, as it did for me around the time of Wade's surprise birthday party. I am now on three antipsychotics, but it took several years to find the right combination.

Now is the best time in history to have a diagnosis. In the past, people were institutionalized because there were no effective medications. Since 1990, medication can work on both the active and passive symptoms. For the first time, people with schizophrenia have the chance to lead a somewhat normal life.

Supportive People

Supportive people, including my mom, my siblings, my phone support team and Wade, have been essential to my wellness. In addition, other supportive people, such as Fay, have appeared at just the right time in my life. Fay appeared when I was searching for a purpose to my life. She inspired me to help in the fight to end the stigma of mental illness by joining the Partnership Program at the Schizophrenia Society.

One day, I asked Fay if I had grown. She laughed and put her hand up to her nose like she was tickled with disbelief that I had asked her such a silly question. "Elizabeth, don't you remember you used to sit at the end of my desk and sleep? We would poke you if you were sleeping too loudly. Mary would cover you up with your coat and I would just say to the people who came into my office to meet with me 'She is alright. Just let her sleep. She is not hurting anything.' And then at 3:30, we would wake you up and send you home." Fay accepts me and the illness and tries to accommodate the needs the illness dictates.

Dr. Margo was supportive and I know she is one of the main reasons I have recovered so fully. Writing the paper for her directed studies course healed my relationship with my mom, but also gave me a sense of self and self-esteem. It was the first time I wrote about myself and put my timeline of experiences all in one place. It is another example of someone who came to my aid just in time. She has helped me be a better daughter, student and person.

My mom, of course, was a main support for me. I am glad that neither of us gave up on our relationship. Like many people do, I had conflicts with my mother. Things were rocky, but I always knew deep down she loved me and that I loved her. She kept connected by giving me plates, she always paid for my university, and we always had fun shopping. In her later years, I would go and visit her at the nursing home and we would eat dinner together. Even though the full healing that took place had not transpired yet, she would listen to my problems and I would come away with hope knowing she was rooting for me. When we did resolve our differences, there was nothing but a sense of peace and comfort, which I still feel when I think about her.

All three of my brothers and their families are supportive people in my life. My brother Doug is the oldest and is the glue keeping our family connected. He, his wife and the rest of his family, make sure we always have nice family get-togethers. Doug and I have regular lunch dates, as well. Dave and his wife live across the country but are only a phone call away. Iain and his wife are always willing to talk about the deep issues of life. Peace in my family relationships is a gift to me.

I am lucky to have other supportive people such as Wade's parents, Dave and Elsie, in my life. They have never judged me, but thought up ways to help me like teaching me how to cook and garden. They have been load lighteners for Wade and I. They always made our times special by cooking a nice meal when we went to visit them in their home in Trochu.

Illness can be tricky to navigate when someone is isolated. It is important to have supportive people to get well and keep well. The people I mentioned above are examples of some of the people who act as my support system and supportive people can be found in different areas of life. Having supportive people can be a kind of first aid when you have problems or need to process experiences. Some people remind you to have fun and not be so results focused; other people understand because they can relate to what you have experienced or know you well enough to give advice.

Knowing people who can help me gives me an emotional safety net. The emotions are real even if the details of the experience may not be. I try to know what I need and am creative about getting my needs met. I have a phone list of people to phone when I need help and everyone knows I have other people to call if they are busy. Different people have different support roles: some provide crisis intervention when I am having a bad day; some give advice in a specific area; and some provide general support. Wade, of course, is supportive at all times and helps me in all areas.

A Reason to Be Well

Wade is my reason to be well. I would like to think that I can be well for my own sake; however, my self-esteem fluctuates and so this is not the case. I need a second reason when I am not feeling well because my motivation to try to stay well can dwindle. At those times, I am able to convince myself it is worth the effort so Wade can have a good life. Lack of motivation is one symptom that makes it hard for me to maintain any momentum. It can be very debilitating when I don't feel like doing something even if it is important to me. Some days, I just don't have the physical or emotional strength to get or keep going. Some days the illness wins and I have learned to just try again the next day and not get upset with myself. Wade reminds me that my efforts have positive effects on our life which helps me want to be well so I can be an equal partner.

I have learned I can have a relapse and then the journey to be well starts all over again. When I am not well I rely on Wade to make decisions for me and need his perspective as a reality check. Wade has always been a central, stabilizing force in my life and I feel the need to try to stay well so the effects of the illness on our lives are minimal and we can have the best life possible. I want him to be proud of me for doing the best I can.

A Reason to Hope

In addition, for me, God has been there through it all; He is the reason I have hope. This book is the way I am serving God, and I have used what I have been through to inform my purpose in life which is what I am asked to do. I want to educate people about mental illness and, perhaps, help people be closer to God. When I talk about my faith, I just say, "I have shopped around and I have found Jesus is the best deal." In my experience, He has always fulfilled his promises to me. Even when I gave up when my mom was in a coma the first time, He answered my prayer for a second chance at our relationship and then over-delivered by completely healing my relationship with my mom before she died. I have been cautioned not to mention God in my story, but if this is my recipe for success, I can't leave out the baking powder that makes the rest of the ingredients work together. I had to do what I could and leave the rest up to God. I also know your beliefs are your business. Everyone has to figure out spiritual matters for themselves.

In my experience, God has slowly earned my trust and in so doing has given me hope because I know whatever I am facing, I am not alone in my struggle. If God really is God then He can do anything, including solve my problems whether big or little. As my spiritual strength has increased, my symptoms have decreased. There is a correlation. God has not healed me completely, but it is much easier to cope knowing that someone has my back. Knowing that God has my back gives me hope.

Something Important To Do

While taking the journey, I found a higher purpose. I needed to make sense of my experiences, and I have found that sharing my story gives my suffering meaning. I share my story through writing and speaking. My start as a real writer came from Heather, Communications Team Lead at my church, who asked me to write stories for the church bulletin. I considered myself a writer for the first time. I have done other writing including some interviews for the church's quarterly magazine. Writing the stories and interviews gave me the skills and confidence to write books.

As well as writing, I enjoy the opportunity to speak. I have been speaking for the

Schizophrenia Society since 1995. I find it is important to talk about my journey if there is ever to be an end to the stigma associated with mental illness. I know what I have learned can ease other people's journey – no matter how they connect with my story. The connections they make and the hints/inspiration/information they take away give my suffering a broader meaning.

Recovery

Schizophrenia is a life-long biological illness of the brain, but recovery is possible. You, or someone you know with a diagnosis, can be mentally healthy in spite of a mental illness. Having a disability, like a mental illness, means that people have unique challenges but they are not insurmountable. All people with schizophrenia are seeking is a good life.

If you know someone who has a mental illness, acceptance is the first step. Accepting the individuals and the illness is an act of giving hope to someone who may have lost sight of their own strength to handle day to day challenges or bigger issues like the "why now?" feeling when symptoms and related difficulties seem to overtake life. Remind them who they are – they are not the illness. Someone who has schizophrenia has been through tough experiences and may have forgotten that they can be well again. Someone can be well even if they experience symptoms at times. Keep a vision of their wellness in mind when interacting with them – it is a gift.

If you have the illness, know there is hope. With the right support and by making wellness the first priority, you have the best chance to be well. My hope is that you will take my recipe and adapt it to your own situation. Remember, being mentally healthy is the journey, not the destination.

Epilogue

The storms of mental illness were not easy to navigate, but over time I learned about myself and how to best manage. Waves of overpowering psychosis and waves of cleansing and wellness make up the rhythm of the illness.

Being mentally healthy while having a mental illness means respecting the illness and recognizing the limitations that come with the diagnosis. Schizophrenia and stress do not mix; adjustments in work life and lifestyle may need to be made. However, establishing new routines and habits that support a simpler lifestyle can be rewarding. I am determined to be as well as I can be. It is a matter of balance.

This journey has given me experiences that are not common, and it has been a real adventure. Although it is not a path I would have chosen, I am happy and hopeful even though I have symptoms.

It is a good life.

Being
Mentally
Healthy
in spite of a mental illness

ADDITIONAL PERSPECTIVES

Symptoms Demystified

According to the Schizophrenia Society, individuals can experience both passive and active symptoms.[5]

Passive Symptoms: characteristics that are reduced or absent in the personality post-diagnosis:

- Flat expression

- Apathy

- Social withdrawal

- Disordered speaking or thoughts

- Diminished ability to start a task and see it through

- Reduction in the ability to find pleasure in life

- Inappropriate behaviour

- Reduced ability to follow social cues (In my experience, one of the most misunderstood symptoms).

Active Symptoms: characteristics that are added to the personality that should not be present post-diagnosis:

- Delusions (fixed false beliefs)

- Paranoia (fear-based thinking)

- Thought broadcasting

- Grandiosity

- Being controlled/controlling

- Movement problems (motionless and clumsy, repetitive actions)

- Hallucination by all five senses (hearing, touch, taste, smell, sight)

Another symptom worth noting is *anosognosia,* a lack of insight into one's own illness because the brain is not able to recognize and react to the fact one is ill (not the same as denial).

(Adapted from Schizophrenia Society Calgary Branch High School PowerPoint Presentation).

Disillumina:
A Day In My Life

My intention in including this section is to offer better understanding of the day-to-day challenges of having a mental illness. Of course, the struggles do not happen for just one day but this type of day has been ongoing since I was diagnosed.

I call the feeling of not being able to discern reality "Disillumina." Disillumina is a name I made up for more extreme incidents in order to cope with them better. I don't trust the world when I am in this state. Schizophrenia is when I see bugs on the floor and I look back and they are not there. Disllumina is when I am fighting with my thoughts and trying to prevent them from going down the road that leads to a break in reality. I live with this from day to day when I am not feeling well....

I am not safe (my first waking thought. Not surprising. It has been like this for a long time).

Shower ... dress ... instant porridge as usual ...

go upstairs for a final check and perfume. Can't smell it (spray, spray no scent). *Someone has been in. They know that I just bought it and now it has no scent. Just another of the hundreds (no, thousands) of things that have happened. Nothing I can do about it ... must get to class.* An uncertainty follows me.

Sit in the back row of the university lecture theatre.

Oh no ... People have decided to sit in this row ... they are doing that to bother me ... If I move they win. If I don't move I will suffer all class long ... what to do ... don't do anything ... I am not going to let other people dictate my behaviour ... People are chatting above the din. I can hear "I'm not glad she is here." "Me neither." "Are you?" "No". *Too many people to just be a coincidence. Must go. Can't leave campus yet ... I have to hand in the response papers to Dr. Finn ... can't wait for class ... I'll go to office hours.*

Waiting outside Dr. Finn's office.

I should take a look at them. Pull out my response papers ...Horror fills my heart

...Oh God they're my rough copies ... He has already given me extra time ... now, I don't have them to hand in ... Someone switched them on me ... I need the ticket stubs. They are with the missing papers ... Dr. Finn said to hand in the response papers to the play with the ticket stubs....

Gone ... I can't replace them

I can't hand it in and then

I will fail the assignment and then

I won't pass the class and then

I won't graduate and then

I'll be a failure and then

It will all have been for nothing.

No. I will not cry. I think sternly. *I'll phone Dr. Brad (my psychologist).*

"Hello, Elizabeth" he answers.

"I want to go home" after explaining my predicament.

"There is a test today, as well." I start to weep. Tears rain down on my papers and I feel like I am in the middle of a rain storm at a bus stop without an umbrella.

"Don't leave until you talk to your professor," he advises.

I see Dr. Finn unlocking his door. After I explain I don't have the response papers to hand in, he suggests, "hand them in later and you can write the exam another time because I'll have a makeup."

"Thank you," I stammer, grateful and relieved because I am not in any shape to write an exam.

Aware that I just barely made it home, I see the papers. They are there. Sitting on the counter. Staring at me. Ticket stubs intact. Disillumina strikes again.

What if I had left without talking to Dr. Finn? I wonder. *I would have failed ... Scary.* Discouraged and disilluminated I make it up the stairs to bed. *I have come this far. I will try to rest ... I remember before this all began I used to be happy. When I met Wade and we got married I thought that I would be happy always. Not to be ... Disillumina came upon me and has tried to take over my life. Now, my life is peppered with fear, doubt and paranoia, a three spice blend that flavours all my experiences.*

I wish it didn't affect my sense of myself. My "I" is something that I am constantly defending against the onslaught of references that try to re-define me. "I" is something that most people aren't consciously aware of and don't think about once they have passed adolescence. My "I" is always in a state of flux. Directions from other sources external and internal eat away at me. Today, one of the hoodies said "Damned." Hopefully not meaning me. Not at all a good day.

It feels safer with my head underneath the blankets. A heavy dark presence invades my space. "Nothing bad is going to happen to you if you listen to me," the dark husky voice says. "Just jump across this small chasm and everything will be okay," he states. In my mind, I see a small distance and can imagine that it wouldn't be hard to jump across. *Sounds reasonable ...* I think hesitantly ... "Just agree with me and your pressure will be relieved," the dark voice insists. *Sounds tempting ... the pressure is unbearable ... I'll try just about anything to not feel this way.* "I'm not trying to play God or anything, but all I need is for you to say yes," the raspy voice pleads. *Play God, eh? I know what this is – it is a trick... God help me – I don't know where you are.*

"Just take my hand and everything will be okay," the husky voice insists.

You are not real, I think alerted to this threat to my sanity. *Do not talk to me again!*

"Come on, take my hand? All I want is your comfort," the voice promises as I feel the chaos of thought trying to take over.

YOU are NOT REAL!!! I fight back as strongly as I can as I struggle to not let go.

"Say you want to be okay," the voice entices.

"No." I squeak aloud. "*I have come too far to lose my way.*

"I am not letting go." I declare.

"How do you know how to say that?!" the voice exclaims as it recedes.

"Come on – just this one time," it tries again.

I did not hear Wade come home from work. Wade interrupts by coming in the bedroom to give me my pills. My head emerges from under the covers and I sit up and take them with a sip of water (sleeping pill and PRN). Sleep comes. I awake the next day.

I am grateful that I have survived a near miss. I was able to fight off psychosis; I did not cross the line. Disillumina did not win this time. Its dark and devious hand has retreated. I don't always see the line and then I am trapped on the other side not able to get back on my own. I wake up knowing that I am safe until the next time. Not knowing the next set of tricks that I will have to navigate is the hard part.

Even though the psychosis was held at bay this time, my biggest fear, which is shared by my friends and family, is that the psychosis will win the battle for my mind and lead to a relapse. The stress of knowing the psychosis can return at any time is ever-present. This is part of the reason that families and friends are also traumatized by the diagnosis a loved one receives.

Trauma and Symptoms

Trauma lingers with the onset of symptoms and symptoms can affect all areas of life.

Physical Health

Symptoms affect my physical health. I have to take vitamins to compensate for the stress that depletes my body of nutrients. When symptoms won't let up, I am tired a lot of the time. I remedy this by getting plenty of rest and clearing my schedule so I have the time and energy for self-care.

Emotional Health

I try not to let myself get caught in "what if" thinking. That road leads nowhere. My emotions always get a work out because the symptoms trigger real emotions. Fear is always lurking and, at times, I can't rationalize it out of my mind and I need medication, someone to talk to and rest.

I tend to deal with the thoughts as they come up because ruminating on what is bothering me tends to make it grow and then it takes up even more space in my mind.

Self-Esteem

My self-esteem fluctuates. At times, I want to give up and at times I am confident that things will work out for me. My conspiracy thoughts centre around someone trying to wreck my life. The biggest lie is that things will never change or get better.

The way I feel about myself is sometimes tied to what other people think of me which can include messages in my environment. For example, I sometimes hear pieces of other people's conversations and I think they know me and are talking about me or a sign I see can disturb me because I think it relates to me and my experiences. It is hard not to take things personally.

I can't believe everything I think and my belief is that not every thought I think is something I have to claim as my own. I have to dismiss thoughts that don't lead me in the direction I want to go. Thoughts of internalized stigma and shame do not serve me and I need to get help from counsellors and loved ones. I sometimes have to ask someone important to me if they still love me. I need confirmation. I need others to tell me I am okay.

Lingering trauma can be as debilitating as the illness. I need to process my experiences in order to get past them. Schizophrenia affects my physical health, my emotional health, and my self-esteem. Remedies involve self-talk, talking to my trusted advisors, medication, vitamins and rest. It takes skills that I have developed over time and a group of good people to help me stay on track and not let the illness win.

Social Role Valorization (SRV)[6]

At Progressive Alternative Society of Calgary (PASC), I was exposed to Dr. Wolfensberger's theory, Social Role Valorization, which helped me accept and work with my disability, and therefore, realize my own value. I was able to overcome the devaluation that comes with the stigma of having a mental illness. The three basic tenets of social role valorization are image, competency, and having a valorized role, which lead to the good things in life.

As I was learning these concepts my own self-worth started to improve dramatically.

My mom made sure I had nice clothes. She understood that this enhanced my image and increased my self-esteem which made others perceive me as competent. Looking like I am at a job interview every day decreases the chance that I will be devalued or treated poorly because of stigma.

My appearance and the competency I had gained from my job at the city later landed me the job at PASC. This increased my self-esteem and gave me a valued role as a worker and income earner. It gave me a sense of belonging and contribution and a higher purpose because I was working in human services providing one-on-one support for adults with developmental disabilities.

At first, I was very uncertain that I could do my job, but I grew into the role and became very competent. This led to increased self-esteem and self-acceptance which enhanced the other roles I occupy.

The valued role of worker gave me more competencies and led to other valued roles: university student; university graduate; writer for the church; and my current role as an author. The valued roles led to valued relationships as I met co-workers, bosses and professors who had a hand in my success.

For me, the ultimate goal of social role valorization is having universally agreed upon good things in life:

- **A job (preferably paid, but unpaid is acceptable).** The job at PASC was the catalyst to my success because I was able to go back to university and have an understanding workplace. The people at PASC understood my disability and knew it was important I accomplish my goals, such as succeeding at university, outside of work.

- **Friends.** I have friends I have met along the way and it is better than the isolation I felt during times when I found it difficult to reach out. When I was not working or volunteering, I did not have any roles that provided contact with people who could break the isolation.

- **A transcendent belief system.** I have a faith that is strong and a source of strength and comfort for me.

- **A voice.** An income is a source of living well and being treated well and having the self-respect to have an opinion. Having money has allowed me to have a say in my life.

- **A home.** Wade and I have always had a decent place to live. Even though a feeling of home does not come easily to me, I know Wade has always tried to provide a safe place for me to be.

- **Opportunities to develop abilities.** I certainly have had opportunities and now I can see the results of the hard work I have put into the opportunities I have been afforded. For example, work, university and being a wife and daughter have all been challenging but I have overcome the obstacles.

- **A basic level of respect.** This may sound like it should be a matter of course but for a person with a disability this is not always the case. I need the people in my life to know or want to know about mental illness, be enlightened and respect my struggle. Healthy relationships, based on respect, have been critical to my success.

- **Individuality.** Individuality means not being grouped and stereotyped which is often the case when someone has a label attached to them. My mother cautioned me to never accept the limitations that come with a label.

- **Ability to contribute and have contributions acknowledged.** Appreciation for effort and contribution is crucial. I felt very supported and encouraged by the people at PASC. I received a ten-year award for my service and I know that my efforts were appreciated.

Being devalued can be a way of life for people who live with the stigma of having a disability, such as a mental illness. I have the good things in life because I have had help with my image. In addition, my skills have developed which led to competencies through a valued role that led to more competencies and more valued roles and relationships. I view my disability through the lens of SRV. The theory provides a framework to understand my disability and make sense of it, and decreases the likelihood I will be devalued. Consequently, I have recovered more fully.

A Word from Deanna

Sometimes, people with schizophrenia need other people to go out of their way and intervene and provide support. Deanna intervened in my life and continues to support me. She made the effort, went out of her way and found me. And her help was very timely even though she did not know that I was in trouble and needed her. After I sent Deanna what I had written about her in the book and told her the book was chosen as recommended reading for one of the university classes in which I had spoken, she sent me an email.

Deanna, who has known me for many years, has seen me at various stages of my journey with mental illness and her message reflects what I have come through and the possibilities that lie ahead.

….I'm honoured by your words, by including me in your books. I guess, in a way, I feel the praise is not justified. You see, God loves us enough to be a "royal nag." It was He who prompted me to make those visits, to make the effort. At times, He gives me no rest until I obey. I know it's for my betterment, the blessing of others and His kingdom and glory, but He just can be such a nag. God nagged, God prepared me, through life's lessons to be equipped to be of some help to you. I can't begin to express the joy I feel being one of the many people who have helped sustain you and thereby been a part of your ministry: a ministry that has already affected at least tens of thousands of people; a ministry that once your book is published could affect millions. I was a teary mess on Sunday, so overjoyed with your good news, so glad that the brokenness of our lives is making a difference. I'm in such awe at the intricacies of God's handiwork. I have endured a lot in order that my faith could mature. You have endured a lot to get to this point. No doubt we will both endure much more before our work here on earth is done but we are blessed – blessed to be able to see that our struggles have not been in vain. We are witnessing the harvest of our labour. Not everyone gets to see that. Again, I'm in such awe of it all.

Your fight for sanity, your struggle to learn how to live well with your illness, for a sense of safety and belonging has no doubt drained your bucket empty but you are living an amazing story, making a positive impact on society. You have a network of loved ones, a church home, and a God who never lets go of your hand, a God who will carry you when you need Him to. We both do. In this case, He nagged me until I found you, and began rebuilding the bridge between us. I could make no other choice at that time. We have free will but God can be very persuasive and compelling.

Moses was a reluctant leader. He made excuses. "I'm not good with words." he said, but Moses had no choice; he had to "Go" and help set God's people free. I had my excuses but in the end I had no choice but to go and help set God's Elizabeth free.

I love you.

Take care.

Deanna

Springboard for Understanding

If you are someone with a mental illness or a caregiver or you want to gain a better understanding of schizophrenia, here are some questions to consider.

1. Pick out one idea or something you learned from each chapter and write it down. What strikes you about the main points now that they are in one place?

2. Make a note of what made you laugh and what made you cry. Ask yourself why you were affected.

3. What bothered you? Why did it bother you? If you are reacting to something in the book, an issue you are not aware of might have been brought to the forefront.

4. What surprised you about Elizabeth's story?

5. What stigmas surrounding mental illness have you noticed?

6. What can you do to reduce the stigma?

7. Do you know someone with a mental illness?

8. Think about how you react to someone with a mental illness?

9. How can you support someone with a mental illness?

10. If you have a mental illness, what suggestions does Elizabeth make that you can integrate into your own life?

And Now, a Word from My Sponsor (Wade)

Elizabeth provided a glimpse into her day-to-day struggles, whether they are with symptoms, motivation or clarity in her thought processes. My chapter is from the perspective of the primary caregiver and provides a sense of what might be expected when living with and supporting a person with Schizophrenia.

After we returned from the honeymoon, everything started to unravel in Elizabeth's world. Elizabeth was having strange thoughts about her friends and people close to us and was thinking someone had been coming into our apartment and stealing our wedding gifts. Being a new husband, I was told by friends there would be a change in both of us as we start our new life together. So with this in mind, I thought she must be having a little trouble adjusting to her new role as a wife. It sounded about right to me! I would make excuses for why she felt the way she did and passed her behavior off as the stress created by being a new wife. It may appear as though I was experiencing some sort of denial. Who would want to think there might be something wrong with their new wife? Certainly not me.

I did not want to wreck a good thing by saying, "You know, honey, you are acting very weird." After three years of dating and deciding to spend the rest of my life with this person, the last thing I wanted to hear was that my wife was not right.

The level of denial grew. During the next year, some of our close friends mentioned to me that they thought Elizabeth was acting a little strange and that she had some thoughts that were not normal in their opinion. I would defend her by saying that they must have misunderstood her or maybe she was trying to make a joke. The symptoms increased and the paranoia escalated. I tried to use logic and reason to combat these symptoms and bring Elizabeth back to reality.

Even after taking Elizabeth to a doctor who agreed her symptoms were from the stress of a new marriage, and that time was all she needed to adjust to her new life as a wife, she did not get better. With the doctor not taking the paranoia and other symptoms seriously, Elizabeth now believed what she was experiencing was real. This caused an enormous amount of conflict in our marriage as the last thing anyone would want to be told is what they are experiencing is not real. Imagine if a friend said "The cup of coffee you just finished was not coffee," or "The empty cup was never filled to begin with!" The immediate response would be tell the friend he or she was crazy. Denial is a very common feeling for caregivers.

When friends say something is not right, try to give them the benefit of the doubt because if they are true friends they're only trying to give their perspective in order to help. Sometimes you need the view of a person looking in from the outside. The sooner your loved one can get help, the better off he or she will be. The longer time passes, the more damage the brain will experience and the longer the recovery process. Please bear in mind everything I am sharing is from my experience; I am not a doctor or psychologist. I'm just an ordinary guy trying to do what's right.

Once my denial had been dealt with, the next step was action. Elizabeth's childhood friend, Deanna, had come to see her and she pulled me aside and told me I must get her to a hospital.

Deanna had already been through a similar situation in her family and recognized all of the signs and symptoms. By now I was at my wits' end and needed to do something quickly. Making the decision to take Elizabeth to the hospital, I believe, was one of the most difficult decisions I ever had to make. I had no idea what was going to happen or how this single action was going to change the rest our lives.

When I took Elizabeth to the hospital my mind was racing. I was so scared because she was very, very sick. There were so many questions that needed to be answered but where could I go or whom could I ask? *What will happen to her? Where will they take her? Will they take her at all? Will she ever get out?* My mind was so full of what ifs, I didn't know if I could follow through with it. But I knew I had to. The only way to get Elizabeth the help she needed and to have any hope of saving my marriage to the woman I loved was to follow through and have her admitted.

The hospital admission process was very traumatic for both of us. When we pulled up to the hospital Elizabeth immediately recognized what was about to happen and bolted from the car before I had even stopped. She ran off very quickly but I did manage to catch her. She was screaming and trying to get away. Two ambulance attendants, thinking I was trying to force her into my car, happened to be outside and ran over to help her. I quickly explained our situation to them and they helped calm her down and take her into the emergency room.

At this point, they split us up and talked to us separately to find out the real story. I felt they thought I was abusing her but I think their view was a result of their training mixed with experience. It doesn't lessen the feeling that they thought I was doing something wrong. I was filled with fear about what Elizabeth was going through in the next room. She was locked in a room, being watched, which had always been a strong part of her paranoia, and feeling like the people she was afraid of had finally had her locked up. In her mind, the people who she thought were bothering her had won.

Once Elizabeth was admitted and settled they said I could go home. The only suggestion they could give me was "go home." I had just committed my wife and all they could say was "go home." Seeing her in the first few weeks in the hospital was very hard for me because she was very heavily medicated and not her usual perky self. The woman I married was spontaneous and vibrant. She always had an opinion on a topic but loved to hear other opinions and respected them whether or not she agreed. But seeing her in this state was devastating to say the least. Where had my Elizabeth gone and would I ever get her back?

When Elizabeth was admitted, no one had helped me with what I needed or told me what I should do. Going to work the day after I admitted Elizabeth and acting like nothing was wrong was so hard. *Do I tell my co-workers I just had Elizabeth committed? How will they treat me? Will they judge us?*

Thinking about my needs and how I was feeling might seem selfish; however, it is important to recognize that what you are feeling is important and it is also important to take care of yourself and learn as much as possible about the illness. My advice is to ask a lot of questions. I didn't because I was completely paralyzed. The most difficult emotion to deal with is the fear of not knowing what's next and how to deal with it. Almost all of the information I did receive was about Elizabeth's illness, not what she was going to need to help her recover or where to turn for help with her recovery. As well, no information was provided to counsel me about my feelings and what I should do to maintain my sanity.

Eventually, Elizabeth was released and I brought her home – but she was not the same. Her thoughts were sad and dark and her feelings seemingly overshadowed our world. She still believed people were trying to drive her crazy. At every turn her paranoia crept into our lives. To help reduce her fear of someone coming into the house, we put security bars on all the windows and doors. This measure was short-lived. Elizabeth had decided the bad people had found a way to get a spare key. Rekeying the locks didn't work either. I was willing to try just about anything to help defend against the paranoia but I could not win. Some of the conspiracies were too tightly wound and there was no way to break in. Yet, as caregivers, we continue to try, because we love the people we care for and we want nothing more than to have our spouse, son, daughter or parent be well.

I wasn't sure I could remain married to Elizabeth as she was. In my mind, I had lost my wife and I was going through a grieving process which was unrecognizable to me because I hadn't lost anyone in my life before. *Could I leave Elizabeth? How would she cope? What would she do?* Struggling with these newfound feelings, I gave myself an out if I needed it. I told myself, *"I will stay with Elizabeth until she is strong enough to handle her own affairs and then I will reassess the situation."* Just the act of saying this took a huge emotional load off of my shoulders because I felt I had an out. But then I had to tell Elizabeth what I had decided. Having this discussion was not an easy task. I did not think it was right to be secretive about life-altering decisions and not tell my spouse.

Elizabeth took the news of my decision very well. However, there was a positive side effect I did not expect. Elizabeth took this as an opportunity to try and get better and work on her illness to improve our marriage so I would want to stay. I felt like

I had regained some sense of control and I could function without this weight on me.

At this point, I was emotionally drained and I realized it was necessary to take care of myself. How can someone care for a loved one if they have nothing left to give? It simply can't be done! Tools and coping mechanisms to help deal with the paranoia and the behaviours related to the symptoms are needed. As I learned, burying myself in work was an epic fail. Having a meaningful hobby can be very therapeutic but how could I have a hobby when she was counting on me? I had to give my brain time to process which required a break from caregiving along with involvement in another activity.

In order to maintain my mental health in this new life, I had to give myself permission to enjoy something. It doesn't matter what it was: walking, running or skiing. It was and is very important to do something for myself.

Auto racing was my hobby of choice. Racing me has given me an outlet to be with like-minded people and to focus 100% on the task at hand. When in a battle for position in a race I cannot afford to let my mind wander; there must be complete focus. This alone gave my brain time to process all of the feelings and emotions I was having.

In addition, I was amazed at how much emotional support I received from friends in the racing community even if they didn't know what I was going through. Sometimes just being around other people who are having a good time is very beneficial. Just because the new role was caregiver, it did not mean there could be no more fun in my life.

At first, I felt a huge amount of guilt simply because I was having fun without Elizabeth and knew she may be at home experiencing a flurry of symptoms and struggling. I had to stay vigilant if I was going to continue to help Elizabeth with her recovery.

Schizophrenia is a terrible illness and has many facets to it. The paranoia can show up in many ways and completely blindside someone. When the symptoms of paranoia occurred it really pissed me off because there was nothing I could do to prevent it.

So many times Elizabeth would become paranoid about something or someone she had seen and I would get so angry. Elizabeth had to endure the continuous pain, suffering and anxiety the paranoia would cause her. I would find myself furious with her because she was having symptoms. *I love her, damn it. How could I feel like this?* It was not her fault; her brain was not functioning normally.

Realizing all of these symptoms were not her fault, I needed to find a way to remove the negative feelings I had toward Elizabeth. It occurred to me that I was mad at the illness and not Elizabeth. The epiphany of being mad at the illness and not at Elizabeth came as a result of allowing myself time away from her and the illness.

The ability to detach the negative emotion from Elizabeth changed everything for me. Now when she is having a bad day or bad symptoms it still bugs me a bit but I have no negative feelings toward her. I only feel caring, compassion and love. Now I can keep a clear head and help her work through her feelings. Being able to work through each episode requires patience and a considerable amount of diligence.

Sometimes you may not be able to help your loved ones understand what they are going through isn't reality. However, just the act of listening to them and believing what they are feeling is real to them is very powerful. Most people in a crisis situation only want to be heard. They aren't necessarily expecting you to have an immediate solution to the symptom.

Elizabeth and I have had countless long discussions about her symptoms. Sometimes the conversations go on for hours and hours. Listening to her and helping her work through her delusion may be all she needs from me at the time. Giving Elizabeth the opportunity to express her feelings helps take the emotional edge off her experiences and reduces the stress. There is no cure for the delusions but with the help of supportive friends, her psychiatrist, her psychologist and proper medications we can manage Elizabeth's symptoms.

Then there are times when Elizabeth may not want to do something and tries to get me to do it for her. I then have to decide if it is a task she is capable of and if it is, I will not do it for her. In order for her to increase her functionality she must take risks. Not every risk comes with success but even so she learns how to cope better from every experience and situation she encounters.

I mentioned I was going to leave when Elizabeth was better. I didn't. At this point, five years had passed and she was well on her road to recovery. We have as normal a life as possible. The reason I didn't leave is I gave myself time to breathe and I remembered something very important to me: my wedding vows. When the minister said to me, "Will you take Elizabeth for better or for worse, in sickness and in health till death do you part?" he didn't mean "except if it's inconvenient for you" now, did he? I had another epiphany. While remembering my wedding vows, knowing that the woman I married was still inside and she was recovering, I decided I was going to stick it out and stay. All I could think was, "Quick. Where's Elizabeth? I have to tell her the news."

There have been some casualties in our relationships with friends. Some friends want little or nothing to do with us now that Elizabeth is ill. Most people have some preconceived notions of what the illness is and are afraid. Unfortunately, most of the time, they are misinformed. All you can do is explain the truth to them and let them decide if they still want to be friends.

On the plus side, a handful of close friends have been so very supportive of both Elizabeth and I. They have helped us deal with many crisis situations and been there regardless of what has happened. You will find out quickly who your true friends are. There will be new friendships made after the diagnosis that will remain strong for years to come because they have been through it too.

The other aspect that surprised me was that I found myself helping families who had recently had a family member diagnosed with Schizophrenia. I'm pleased I can share my experience with Elizabeth's recovery with others to help them cope as caregivers and perhaps give some insight into the illness.

I don't think of Elizabeth as a Schizophrenic; she is not her illness. She is a person with Schizophrenia. People with Schizophrenia do not want sympathy. All people with an illness – regardless of what it is – deserve empathy for their plight and respect for their courage. The support that is needed is to help give clarity to tasks and situations that people with Schizophrenia may face in their day-to -day lives.

There are times when Elizabeth will get stuck and not know how to deal with something and really all that she needs is a sounding board to help her through it. Supposedly "healthy" people take this for granted and find it difficult to understand that some people cannot do this for themselves. I have learned just how much to push Elizabeth and how much to let her fall and when to try and insulate her from a situation as a way of managing the illness.

Dealing with the illness and the many emotional triumphs and the defeats take time and patience but, as caregivers, we can never give up! I think there are times when I wonder if I'm cut out for this. But in the times you are so upset at the illness and the symptoms, you have to remember the good times you have experienced and keep them as a goal. Elizabeth has done some incredible work on her emotional wellbeing and discovered much about herself and how she thinks about her life and her relationships. These discoveries have led to her healing the negative feelings associated with each of the situations that caused emotional turmoil. Elizabeth has done all the work; I have only provided a safe environment for her to accomplish these tasks.

I'm so proud of her!

Endnotes

1. Barry Broadfoot, Ten Lost Years, 1929 -1939: Memories of Canadians who Survived the Depression (Toronto: McClelland & Stewart Doubleday Canada, 1973).

2. Nancy Friday, My Mother/My Self: The Daughter's Search for Identity, (New York: Bantam Doubleday Dell Publishing Group. Inc., 1987), 69.

3. Ibid, 333.

4. Ibid, 241.

5. Schizophrenia Society of Alberta, Calgary Chapter. *Calgary Branch High Schools Presentation* 2012.

6. Wolf Wolfensberger, Susan Thomas and Guy Caruso, "Some of the Universal 'Good Things of Life' which the Implementation of Social Role Valorization Can be Expected to Make More Accessible to Devalued People," The International Social Role Valorization Journal 2, no. 2 (1996): 12-14.